Hydroponic Gardening

HYDROPONIC GARDENING

The 'magic' of modern hydroponics for the home gardener

By Raymond Bridwell

Lecturer, Loma Linda University Extension
International Consultant in Hydroponics

WOODBRIDGE PRESS PUBLISHING COMPANY
Santa Barbara, California 93111

Published by
WOODBRIDGE PRESS PUBLISHING COMPANY

Post Office Box 6189
Santa Barbara, California 93111

World Rights Reserved

Library of Congress Catalog Card Number: 72-86151

International Standard Book Number: Hard Cover, 0-912800-00-3
Soft Cover, 0-912800-09-7

Published simultaneously in the United States and Canada

Printed in the United States of America

Fourth Printing

Enjoyable, Carefree Gardening

- a foreword by EDDIE ALBERT

I really believe we would all be a lot better off if we could spend more time with green, growing plants; growing some of our own food; being closer to nature.

The trouble is, it is pretty hard for most of us to do that, geared as we are to city life.

What Raymond Bridwell has done in his new book is to show us a way to create our own satisfying "green acres" in the limited space we have.

I was amazed when I studied a chart on Page 120 showing how much food you can produce, year-round, in a little greenhouse only about eight-by-twelve feet in size.

And when you realize that Mr. Bridwell is talking about modern hydroponic techniques, that means your gardening is almost carefree. The plants are fed a naturally-balanced solution of nutrients right on schedule; and, since they are protected in this nearly perfect environment, you don't have to fight bugs and weeds—or the weather.

The practical methods explained in this book will help you to do your gardening with a lot more relaxation and enjoyment and a much greater return of nutritious food.

I hope you feel as I do that helping plants to grow and eating food you have produced with your own efforts will make your life a lot more pleasant—and maybe save you a lot of money, too!

This book should make it much easier for you to do all that. I enjoyed reading it and I hope you do, too.

Raymond Bridwell, "friend of living things."

About the Author

THE AUTHOR HAS a feeling about plants—about plants as living organisms. They need nourishment. They need air and light; protection from disease and a hostile environment.

But Raymond Bridwell believes they also need tender loving care—just as people do. They need a gentle touch and a friendly attitude. The author believes plants flourish under the hand of one who relates to them as one organism to another—both a part of God's creation.

When he goes further and says he finds plants responsive, appreciative of this attitude in human beings, it is hard to disbelieve him. His thirty-year record of success as a "friend" of plants speaks for itself.

His hydroponically-produced fruits and vegetables are in great demand for their outstanding appearance, flavor, and nutritive value. While some horticulturalists bemoan the problems of greenhouse gardening, Raymond Bridwell goes right ahead with flourishing production—virtually disease-free and insect-free.

One cannot consider plants alone, he believes. They exist in an environment that includes other plants, people, insects and other animate creatures, to say nothing of the elements. This total environment affects the plant's performance as a living thing and must be taken into account by the successful gardener. The author helps the reader of this book to do just that.

Raymond Bridwell's lifetime in agriculture is broadly based. It includes years of service as nurseryman, farmer, commercial gardener, floral gardener, seedsman and propagator, tree farmer, landscape designer, compost manufacturer and distributor.

Among his educational attainments, he has a degree in anthropology and has specialized in the study of prehistoric agriculture, a study he believes is of great value to the gardener today.

The author's experience in hydroponic gardening goes back to its modern beginnings in the late 1930's. He is today not only a successful commercial hydroponic grower, but also a sought-after lecturer, university instructor, and consultant.

The reader will certainly benefit from his advice as a gardener. We believe that he will also benefit from an acquaintance with Raymond Bridwell as a sensitive, intelligent, and stimulating human being.

—Howard B. Weeks, Ph.D.

Acknowledgements

EVERY BOOK REPRESENTS the combined talents and knowledge of many persons and this one is no exception. I wish to thank for their encouragement and assistance Dr. Vernon H. Koenig and others at Loma Linda University, including Dr. Andrew N. Nelson and Jacob R. Mittleider. I also extend my sincere appreciation to those students and friends who have assisted in providing illustrations and other important material for the book.

No less contributors to this work are those who through the years have inspired the author in his study and experimentation in agriculture. My wife, Hazel Bridwell, certainly is foremost among these; but I also owe much to such persons as W. D. Humphrey of Phoenix, Arizona; Dr. Tony J. Ganje of the department of soil science and agricultural engineering at the University of California at Riverside; and Dr. Leon Bernstein of the United States Salinity Laboratory in Riverside, California.

My grateful thanks to all of these and more who have enhanced my own learning process as well as those who have assisted directly in the preparation of this book.

—The Author

9

Raymond Bridwell's multiple-session university extension courses are always well attended, attracting a wide variety of people—businessmen, housewives, professional people, young people—who want to make gardening a healthful pleasure, the hydroponic way.

Contents

Hydroponic Gardening

Chapter 1

Hydroponic Gardening:

for new success, pleasure, and good health

WHATEVER YOUR PREVIOUS experience in gardening, I know you will be interested if I can show you how you can economically produce enough fruit and vegetables for your family with only 15 to 20 minutes of work per day. These fruits and vegetables can be superior in appearance, flavor, and nutritive value (my own produce, for example, brings unusually good prices in gourmet markets). They can also be disease-free, grow faster, and have far better keeping qualities than most fruits and vegetables.

I want to show you how to accomplish this, conveniently, year-round, in as little space as a 10- by 12-foot area of your backyard — through modern, automated hydroponic gardening.

Revival and Refinement

Actually, modern hydroponics is a revival and development of methods that go back almost 300 years. Many of the materials used today were formulated more than a hundred years ago by scientists in Germany.

What has generated such an interest in hydroponic gardening today? Think of the increasing air pollutants that damage not only human beings but also vegetation. Think of the proliferation of diseases, and insects and other pests that can be controlled in conventional agriculture only at great ecological cost. And how can one help but think of the soaring prices of fruits and vegetables every time he enters a supermarket — to say nothing of the inevitable deterioration in quality between farm and store and home?

No wonder modern hydroponics is booming—when it can eliminate most of the environmental hazards; when it can emphasize the natural factors in superior plant growth; when it can be such a convenient, economical method of producing one's own supply of super-fresh, super-quality fruits and vegetables.

Let's find out what it's all about and how you can do it.

A Concise Definition

Hydroponics, simply defined, is the growing of plants in a solution of the nutrients necessary for plant growth, rather than directly in the soil.

A rich variety of superior fruits and vegetables may be grown
simultaneously and continuously in modern hydroponic gardening.

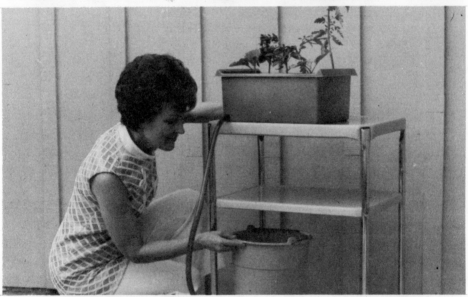

Hydroponics is a principle. It can be applied on simple or complex levels. Here is a very small, but very efficient indoor hydroponic "garden"—a plastic utility tub half-filled with clean gravel and with a plastic pail of nutrient solution connected by a short piece of plastic hose. Twice a day, Dorothy Weeks raises that pail (it can be placed on a stool or shelf) to allow the solution to run into the tub (to just below the surface of the gravel) by gravity flow. After a few minutes, the bucket is lowered and the solution drains back for reuse. It works.

The author confers with student, William J. Haas, in his sophisticated home hydroponic greenhouse. Controls, described in this book, automatically regulate pumps, fans, coolers, heaters for optimum growing conditions and superlative food production.

Naturally, the roots cannot remain constantly in the solution—lack of air, for one thing—so there has to be a means of periodic application of nutrients, followed by exposure to air.

Typically, this is accomplished by growing the plants in an inert medium, such as gravel. Nutrient solution is applied at regular intervals, then as it drains away from the growing medium, air comes into contact with the roots.

But then you have lost that nutrient solution. So the next step is to place the growing medium, the gravel, in a tray approximately nine inches deep, from which the solution can be recovered as it drains away. Then it can be used again, and again, and again—with occasional checking to maintain its proper nutritive balance.

Now, place this solution in a tank, attach a pumping mechanism with timing and temperature controls, and you have automated the feeding of your garden. Just relax and watch it grow!

A Controlled Environment

But there is still the outside climate and the polluted atmosphere, pests, and diseases that come with it. So the next step is to control the environment by enclosing your growing trays and nutrient circulating system in a small greenhouse. There are some excellent greenhouses on the market and I would strongly recommend one of these, professionally designed and constructed; although if one has the know-how and the time there is no reason why he could not build his own. My experience, however, is that the do-it-yourself procedure in greenhouse construction may often actually cost more in the long run.

For year-round production, the greenhouse should have some means of internal heating and fans for air circulation. With thermostat and humidity controls, your garden is truly automated.

Since you are bringing the nutrients to the roots, rather than forcing the roots to range far and wide in the soil looking for nutrients, far less growing space is needed than in a conventional greenhouse garden. Therefore, a hydroponic greenhouse about 10 feet by 12 feet can contain enough plants, growing in trays, utilizing overhead space by means of stakes and strings for the climbing plants—to provide all the fresh fruits and

On a commercial scale, hydroponic gardening is providing superior fruits and vegetables for discriminating customers as well as solving food problems in many parts of the world—from Finland to Israel to Africa to New Guinea. Modern hydroponics, through good sanitation, avoids the problems often encountered in ordinary greenhouse gardening while capitalizing on its advantages of environmental control and automated feeding procedures.

vegetables you need: tomatoes, strawberries, chard, cucumbers, melons, squash, beans, okra, corn—and many, many more.

Part of a World Program

What we are talking about here is not just a plaything, but the real thing. It is gardening—far more concentrated and productive than is possible by conventional practices, and with a more beautiful and nutritive product. But it is also a system of food production which on a larger scale is helping to solve some of the critical food problems of the world.

We are going to discuss in detail how you can do this kind of gardening in your own backyard—or even on a terrace or rooftop for that matter—but let's take the time right here to look at the global implications of hydroponics, so that you can know that your new role as a hydroponic gardener makes you a part of a program with real significance to the future of human life on this planet.

In addition to large scale commercial operations in this country—like mine in southern California, and others —investigators in other parts of the world, spurred by great concern for world food needs, and by evidence of the outstanding quality, flavor, and appearance of hydroponically-grown food, have been developing projects in many countries.

A friend of mine recently returned from a visit to oil-rich but soil-poor and water-poor Kuwait; a visit made at the invitation of the Kuwait government. He declared hydroculture to be ideally suited to the conditions there.

Lush, year-round vegetable production in greenhouses is commonplace in many European countries.

The United Nations is providing funds for a pilot operation in Lebanon to be built and staffed by hydro-culture personnel. This will be the forerunner of major projects in other Middle East lands. After all, because of the recycling of the nutrient solution, hydroponics uses only one-thirtieth the water of conventional gardening.

For many years in Israel a great deal of work has been done in hydroponics. Just before World War II, water-culture experiments were begun in Naharia. Sand-culture methods have also been used as the science has developed over the years.

New Promise in the Promised Land

The development of hydroponics in Israel received additional stimulus from unique religious factors. Because of observance of the Sabbatical year, in which the land is left fallow every seventh year, some Israeli settlements tackled the problem of producing fresh vegetables during that seventh year. Gravel-culture programs begun in 1952 at Kibbutz Hafetz-Hayim, suggested that—religious factors aside—hydroponic culture might be an economical agricultural method in Israel.

Similar experiments and developments may be reported in such differing places as New Guinea, Iceland, the Philippines, Sicily, Japan, and throughout Europe.

New Hydroponic Plant Varieties

Besides experimentation with methods, there is also experimentation with new varieties of produce especially developed for hydroponic gardening.

In fact, it is expected that many such varieties of

This grower in Finland produces high-quality fruits and vegetables.

produce will surpass any ever grown before. There is under development, for example, a new low-acid tomato as well as a cucumber that will agree with almost every type of digestive system.

How do hydroponically-grown foods compare with soil-grown foods? If a *perfectly ideal* soil could be found for each *individual plant,* probably nothing would surpass such a soil-grown food.

However, that is an ideal rarely attained even with the most persistent effort. The facts are that hydroponically-grown foods are richer than almost all their soil-grown counterparts if they are properly grown—as I am going to show you how to do in this book. In the hydroponic process everything can be used to provide nature at its best, with regularity. The superior nutritive value of hydroponic produce has definitely been established by laboratory analysis.

Most failures in conventional gardening are due to what? Lack of knowledge, perhaps; but what else? Poor soil, insects, weather, diseases, moisture problems. All of these can be overcome by hydroponics. You can furnish

Marvelyn Sturtevant (holding nine-month-old Allison), together with her husband, Dr. Rolland Sturtevant, manage to keep up a busy professional and social life, provide tender loving care for three small children, and operate a successful hydroponic garden all at the same time. In fact, the healthful food produced in that greenhouse is really part of the tender loving care of those children! This 10- by 12-foot greenhouse is a "package" like those available from various suppliers.

Mrs. Sturtevant herself is amazed at the size and color of a bumper crop of cucumbers in her hydroponic greenhouse. Utilization of vertical space permits the production of a remarkably large quantity of fruits and vegetables.

the plant with the nutrients it needs, exactly what it needs, when it needs it. You can protect it from disease. You can protect it from wind. You can use a very small area, concentrate the production, and get predictable results.

This makes possible a large list of vegetables fresh from growing tray to you. We mentioned some of them. All those I have mentioned could be grown in a greenhouse measuring 10 by 12 feet.

One gentlemen I have talked to within the last few months suggests that in a 10- by 12-foot greenhouse, with a minimum expenditure of time each day, you can reap a harvest of approximately $50 worth of produce every month, to say nothing of its superior qualities. This is hydroponics. We want the most out of what we do.

We are tired of planting a hundred acres of corn and see the wind blow half of it away. The bugs take half of what is left and when you finally get a harvest the rats and the mice are going to divide that. I don't like that kind of farming.

Years ago I helped my uncle in summer on the ranch and that's the kind of farming we did then. I have no use for it. I would much rather protect the plants a bit and get back what I put into them and more.

An Open-Minded Approach

In considering hydroponics, it may be said that we should suspend tradition and take a fresh, clean look at the way things grow. Many things that you are familiar with in the field growing situation will appear in an entirely different light when they are looked at inside a hydroponic greenhouse. Do not let emotions become mixed with your gardening. There are some things that just have to go. For example, you can't say that just because a particular plant has been growing outside a long time, it can be brought into a greenhouse now in order to protect it. It may be harboring something that will get the rest of the plants in the greenhouse, once and for all.

Long-held opinions will often make a person inhibited and outdated. But I know you want to have the benefit of a fresh look at what is going on today in agriculture, and learn from nature and from other people.

Yes, with hydroponics it is possible for you to be successfully growing vegetables faster than ever before and with predictable results.

There is still another reason I like hydroponic gardening—especially if one thinks of gardening as a kind of relaxation and recreation, a way to work off tensions. I'll tell you that in a conventional garden it is sometimes just as easy to generate tensions as to relieve them! Sometimes an outdoor garden is indeed a lot of frustration, isn't it? One question comes to your mind: Why did I ever start this mess? Because with a little neglect it can get to be a real mess. The outdoor garden can't water itself, can it? It can't weed itself; it can't swat at the insects. But in a hydroponic unit all of this is done for you and your 15 to 20 minutes a day can be really pleasant relaxation.

As a matter of fact, you can't even care for a 10- by 12-foot garden outdoors with just 20 minutes a day, can you? Because it can't be automated.

In Good Company

So you are about to become a hydroponic gardener. You are in great company. Gloria Swanson, the timeless actress and ageless health enthusiast, has made the statement that every hospital should consider having a hydroponic garden, perhaps on its roof, so patients can have the benefit of fresh, tempting, nutritious, and poison-free food. I couldn't agree more.

Don't wait to get yours in the hospital. In just three weeks you can be eating your own succulent varieties of lettuce, and in 90 days you can have a tomato that smells as good as it tastes. The skin is "soft as butter" so there is no need of peeling. Are you ready to go? Then let's begin by looking briefly at some background information.

Mother Earth

Chapter 2

Mother Earth:

source of nutrients

LIKE ALL OTHER means of growing plants, hydroponics is based on supplying the nutrients needed for growth (along with proper aeration, light, temperature, humidity, and other factors, of course). The nutrients for every kind of agriculture are originally in the soil.

The plant produces seed for one purpose. What is that seed looking for when it germinates and sends a root down? We could say water, or a foothold; but mainly the seed is looking for something to use for reproduction. It is going to produce some more seed. So, what those roots are after is nutrients for reproduction.

"Miners of the soil." The primary function of plant roots is to search out and provide to the plant the water and nutrients necessary for growth and reproduction. In hydroponic gardening, nutrients are regularly and consistently presented to the roots. There is no need for them to wander over large areas searching for nutrients that, after all, may not be in the soil. Thus, in hydroponics, planting space can be used more efficiently and all necessary nutrients can always be available to the plant.

What kind of nutrients do they have to have? Why don't they just find nitrogen, potassium, and phosphate? They need balance—at least 16 elements in all. The roots are looking for nutrients in a water solution that they can draw up and supply to the plant in the form of raw building material.

You probably know that a plant can utilize only about five percent of its nutrients in the same form in which it finds them. Ninety-five percent of those nutrients have to be converted by the plant itself into usable form.

Bringing Nutrients to the Roots

Why hydroponics? To help the plant, to help the roots to find the necessary nutrients quickly and easily—to put everything into a solution the roots can "mine" for the elements the plant needs.

According to the Biblical story there was a time when plants were watered from subsurface sources and elements were evenly distributed—the same as in hydroponics. Perhaps, then, hydroponics is as old as the earth!

Well, those elements may have been evenly distributed at one time, but today they certainly are not. We mine nitrates in Chile. We mine phosphates in Canada. Incidentally, do you know how precious phosphate is? We have almost come to believe that phosphate is just messing up the ecology. The fact is, you would be dead without it. Actually, we think so highly of phosphates that in Canada, some $7,000,000 was spent in order to get a phosphate mine into operation. Most of the money was spent to build and operate machines to freeze the permafrost so they could cut through it, put in the head of a shaft, and go in to mine the phosphates.

Now, that is essentially what the root of the plant is doing for you. It is penetrating the soil, mining all the minerals needed for food production.

Whose responsibility is it to see that something is there to mine? It is yours, isn't it? Perhaps we have all realized that more clearly at some time when we planted a garden that didn't turn out so well!

Of course, when we have growing problems it is not always that the seed and its roots do not find nutrients. What else may be involved in our results? Temperature is one thing. Other factors are light, moisture, the wind, even too much of certain nutrients, or bacteria on the roots, allowing a nematode or something to cut the life-line of a particular plant.

Now when I talk about minerals, am I talking only about the nutrients conventionally thought of as such? No. I am also talking about water. It is one of the most precious "minerals," one of the primary "minerals" that human beings mine—in wells, for example. It is one of the main things the plant has to mine for its own use as such as well as because it is the vehicle by which other minerals are carried to the plant—in solution.

All Nutrients from the Earth

So, whatever forms our gardening may take—hydroponic, organic, conventional, we have to recognize that all plants are dependent upon the minerals of the earth. Mother Earth is a depository of minerals. Fertilizers are minerals, coal and petroleum are minerals, water is a mineral. In hydroponics we use water solutions of these minerals as the most consistent and convenient way to present them to the plant.

Good compost should provide the nutrients needed by plants; minus, hopefully, disease organisms that could harm the plants. The nutrients in a naturally balanced hydroponic solution can be the same elements found in good humus with no disease agents at all. All plant nutrients, in whatever form, are originally in the earth.

After all, what is compost made of primarily? Carbon, potassium, any of the minerals you want to mention are in there—or should be if it's a good compost.

What is coal? It's actually an ancient compost peat. If you have access to a very old gardening encyclopedia it will tell you how to use coalslack in gardening. What does coal smell like when we burn it? Sulphur. What else? Ammonia. There's some of that there, too. What else? Humic and folic acids. And they bear lots of nutrients.

Petroleum plays a very important part in all agriculture. Grease for the tractor, insecticides and germicides (petroleum is the base for these), fuel, fertilizer, and synthetics. Are those synthetics made from petroleum basically different from the essential, usable minerals I would get from chicken manure? No, not really; because they, too, came from the vegetable matter and the animal residue that comprised the original material from which petroleum was made.

Look up a dictionary definition of humus. Humus is what we want from a compost pile, isn't it? Humus is simply the organic portion of soil: animal and vegetable residue. Now tell me about that petroleum. What was it? Animal and vegetable residue—organic material, humus.

Nitrates Are Essential

Now for a while right here, let's talk about ecology. And let's talk about how the farmer is supposed to have messed up the ecology with nitrates. He alone certainly hasn't done it. True, nitrate is very difficult to get out of water, but human waste has lots of nitrates, hasn't it?

Forty-five percent of the solids in urine are proteins which break down into ammonia, which break down into nitrite, which breaks down into nitrate. And all the recycled water or reclaimed water has to carry the nitrate if you can't get it out. What about our big dairy farming areas? They inevitably produce nitrates in the surrounding water supply.

But this isn't something new or attributable alone to human activity. There are sections of the White River in Missouri where beautiful water runs down over the gravel—but you'd better not drink it. Nitrates are in it. And there were nitrates in it before there was ever a city close to the river. Where did those nitrates come from? They came from water draining through the caves full of bat guano—which has the highest concentration of nitrate of all natural products. Those same caves produced a great deal of nitrates for gunpowder during the Civil War, incidentally.

All Organic Minerals Related

Let's talk just a bit more about ecology, and the interrelation of all organic materials. We can put a ton of cow manure along with carbon monoxide in a vessel that will stand 900 pounds pressure per square inch. This produces a temperature of around 1,100° Fahrenheit. What is the product, in time? Three barrels of oil and some water.

In LaVerne, California, a similar experiment produced petroleum from ordinary city garbage, under heat and pressure. McAnally Egg Enterprises in Yucaipa, California, has produced oil from chicken manure.

So let's consider the earth a depository of related organic minerals. The Indians call the earth their mother. The earth is your mother. I guess we could say, too, that the ocean is a part of the earth. There you find the trace elements in great abundance. Some of them are active in plant life in ways we do not as yet understand.

Hydroponics and Ecology

We were talking about water as one of the minerals of the earth. Here, hydroponics has great ecological importance. It takes a thousand pounds of water to produce one pound of alfalfa. Now, remember that in hydroponics you are using only one-thirtieth the water it would take to grow the same plants outdoors. Why? Because we are recycling it. It may interest you to know that a commercial greenhouse 32 feet wide and 120 feet long containing a thousand tomato plants uses far less water than would normally be used by a five-member family.

That is why the water has to be analyzed; so we can know precisely what nutrients to add to it. Remember that minerals in the earth are salts. All nutrients are in the form of salts whether they are acid or base minerals. Remember also that most of the crust of the earth, in which most of the growing minerals are found, is silica. Much of the crust of the earth contains salts very conducive to plant growth.

More Efficient Use of Water and Minerals

In many soil structures, however, the water is not available to plants at all and thus the minerals are not either. They are "locked" in the soil. In hydroponics the water and the minerals are always available and we are going to recycle them for thrift and for consistent food production.

Thus, when it comes to minerals in hydroponics, a little extra money spent for the very best goes a long way. Some people build the finest greenhouse, make certain of having the best water and the best of seed. But they will sometimes try to save money on cheap minerals. They are not getting their money's worth. In the large commercial greenhouse I just mentioned, the difference between the best nutrients you can buy and the cheapest is only about $50 a year.

Gravel a Form of Soil

What about natural soil in comparison with the gravel or other growing media used in hydroponics? You know the earth's surface is composed primarily of "rocks," don't you? Large masses of rock, large boulders and

The earth's crust is made up primarily of particulate matter—grit, sand, gravel, rock.

stones, on down to small stones, gravel and grit. Have you ever picked up any clay or silica—something that appeared to be somewhat slick—put it between your teeth and bitten on it? You don't like the idea, do you? Almost invariably we find that the material is actually composed of tiny bits of grit. Now is a tiny bit of grit basically different from a rock as big as a truck? No. It is just smaller.

So remember, the earth's crust is made up primarily of *particulate* matter. And that particulate matter, or matter of small particles, is primarily silica. The earth's crust is composed of about 95 percent silica.

Thus the earth's surface is made up largely of varying sizes of "rock." Mixed with that rock will usually be water and some plant or animal residue.

Measurement of Nutrients

The top six inches of soil can be referred to as the furrow slice. And that top six inches of soil in one acre weighs a little over 2,000,000 pounds. Now two pounds of soil out of the top six inches in an acre is one part per million in that acre. It is this kind of minute measurement we use in analysis of the nutrient content in the soil—for any kind of soil gardening. We use the same kind of measurement for nutrient analysis in hydroponic gardening.

The subsoil is right below that six-inch furrow slice. The subsoil may be rocky or it may be very fine—sometimes to a depth of 20 feet. What is the purpose of the subsoil? It is a water reservoir. It is also the storage area for the minerals your plants will try to find. Remember that we described plants as "miners."

And where do the plants, the roots, go? They go anywhere the soil is friable. Some people pick up some soil, squeeze it in their hand, smell it, throw it back, and tell you what kind of soil it is. Folks, that's pure ceremony. I can do that all day long and I can't tell you what kind of soil it is. I can tell you if it is thick; I can tell you if it's gritty. I can tell you if it smells good, or if it smells sour. But I cannot tell you what's in that soil except by what? Analysis.

So when people tell me what a terrific piece of ground they have, I think they mean they can plow it. I think they grew a crop on it with which they were pleased.

Gravel an Excellent Medium

So now when we talk about the various types of growing media, does gravel look a little better and more logical to you? Why? Because you have expense to think about for one thing. You have to pay for the ground you use. You buy it, rent it, or lease it. And the fellow who sells you farmland or gardenland is often selling it because he hasn't been too successful the last two or three years. You may have a lot of soil building to do.

But with gravel as a growing medium, with all the nutrients in a water solution, you have "soil" that is inexpensive, consistent, controllable. What does soil mean, after all? It simply means a growing medium for plants. Rich soil would mean one that has good particle size with a lot of good nutrients in it.

Do you wonder about earthworms and the soil? I want to state positively that you don't have good soil because you have earthworms. You have earthworms because you have good soil. There are lots of nutrients

Three-eighths-inch gravel, sterilized of all harmful disease agents, is the medium of choice in hydroponic gardening. It provides plant support, retains nutrient solutions for plant use, provides good aeration of roots, and is easy to handle and to change when necessary.

for them to eat. If there were not, the earthworms would move on. They are quite migratory, looking for what they want to eat. They do help in soil aeration, a function actually performed more thoroughly by hydroponic methods.

More for Your Money

In considering soil gardening versus hydroponics as a growing method, it becomes at some point a question of economics. Do you think it is possible for me to spend $200 per acre per year on soil and grow produce profitably? Sometimes I have, in fact, paid that much for an acre of ground. But believe me, whatever you are growing, you had better be growing pretty well. Even though that $200 includes water, you had better be doing a terrific job. You have to have as much automation as you can get. Even if you can find the labor, you can't always afford it.

What other things do you have to have in your favor? You have to have a low power bill, don't you? You have to have a low inventory on equipment. You have to have a low inventory on buildings.

What I have discovered is that I can go to the smaller space, the smaller areas of hydroponic units, intensify the yield of a high-priced or out-of-season crop and economically get the income or produce I need.

Success in Hydroponics

We have been tremendously successful with many varieties of fresh, superior fruits and vegetables that will bring premium prices if you want to sell them—or you can enjoy them in true gourmet style in your own home.

Stay with me now while we talk about the importance of water and nutrient solutions in producing these very special fruits and vegetables. Then we will go on to talk about growing media, greenhouse construction, and other practical matters. Next: Water, the most precious of "minerals" and its conversion to nutrient solutions for your plants.

Water

Chapter 3

Water :

carrier of life

I WANT TO GIVE you a little background on water: where it comes from, how it travels through the soil, how to have it analyzed, and how it affects plant growth. But remember that all through this discussion, I am getting to one major concern in hydroponics—plant nutrients, balanced in solution for optimum utilization by the food plants in your growing trays.

Let's start with water as rainfall. When that water hits the ground, what happens? First, there's a bit of runoff, isn't there? But then what happens to the water as it goes down through the soil into the water table? We hope that some of the "impurities" are filtered

Water for all plant growth comes originally from rainfall. This very "wet" water, with its carbonic acid, drives harmful mineral salts down into the subsoil while adding to the topsoil various elements favorable to plant growth. Only as minerals, nutrients, are in a water solution are they available to the plant—whether the plant roots are in the soil or in a hydroponic growing medium like gravel.

out, don't we? But not just to make the water drinkable. We also want the ground to filter out of the water all the beneficial soluble minerals and store them for plant growth—carbon and sulphur, for example. We also want to leach out of the ground some of the salts that are not beneficial.

Once at a college where I had a landscaping and maintenance responsibility, we had some torrential rains that had us worried about erosion of the lawns. But you know what? Although we hadn't previously been complimented much on the grounds, within about six weeks everyone was commenting on their beauty—how green the trees were, and the grass. Why? Was it what we were doing? No, it was in spite of what we were doing. What happened? The heavy rains leached out the salt that had been inhibiting plant development.

Rainwater is an excellent solvent. It is a very "wet" water, because it includes carbonic acid. It will actually push some of the alkalis and sodium down into the substrata where they belong.

Water "Mined" by Plants

How does water get out of the soil? It evaporates, we can pump it out, or it appears as springs—or even as steam in some places where there is underground thermal activity.

How else does water come out of the soil? Well, those little "miners" we were talking about bring it up—the plants. At times, in the early morning, you can actually see this water "pumped out" by plants in the form of droplets of water around the edges of leaves. We call it transpiration.

The character of the water "mined" by the plants is very important in any kind of gardening and especially so in hydroponics.

The pH of Water

The pH of the water is of major importance; it greatly affects plant growth. The symbol pH represents a measure of the concentration of hydrogen ions per liter of water and thus a measure of the acid-alkaline balance of the water. This balance is often unfavorable in the natural water supply of the area. But the pH of water can readily be changed for use in hydroponics. First, however, you need to know what the present pH is. The higher the concentration of hydrogen ions, the more acid; the lower the concentration, the less acid. Below 7.0 may be considered acid; above 7.0, alkaline. Your water supply source can tell you what the pH of your water is, although it does vary from time to time.

There are several simple kits on the market for testing the pH of your water. One involves the use of Nitrazene tape. There is also a kit utilizing a chemical that you drop into a sample of your water. In each case, either the tape or the water changes color. You then compare the color with those on a chart indicating the approximate pH. You can use both systems, in fact; one as a check on the other. You may also purchase a meter costing about $185, if you wish.

By whatever method, the pH of your water, the the nutrient solution you are using in hydroponic growing, should be checked every four days.

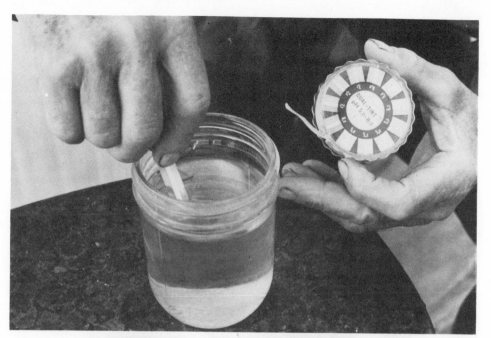

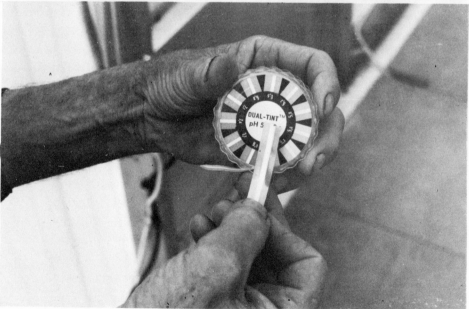

The pH (acidity-alkalinity balance) of the water and the nutrient solution used in hydroponic gardening is important and should be checked every four days. One or more methods can be used, one as a check on another. A good pH range for growing a variety of vegetables simultaneously is between 6.0 and 7.0. Above, Nitrazene tape is dipped into a sample of the nutrient solution. The tape changes color and is then matched with a scale to indicate the approximate pH.

How do you relate to a pH reading? What do you do to the water as a result of it? Well, if your pH measuring device indicates a pH of just below 7.0, you could say the water or solution was relatively neutral as to acidity-alkalinity.

Now what do you do to it? Add acid? Perhaps just a little, in order to make it slightly more acid than alkaline. Three drops of acid in a quart of water will drop the pH one half a point. I use a sulphuric concentrate; very carefully.

If we drop 7.0 pH water to 6.5, that should be suitable for a fairly wide variety of plants. However, if you are growing a single crop hydroponically, you should remember that some plants are typically acid-loving and some are alkaline-loving and adjust the pH to suit the crop you are growing. Here we are talking about a balance in which a variety of garden crops can flourish.

Water Analysis

In hydroponics you need to know more about your water supply than just the pH, however. You need to know its present total composition so you will know what to add to it in order to create the best nutrient solution for the prize food plants you are going to grow.

No matter what your past experience with water has been in conventional gardening, you must have a thorough knowledge of its characteristics for successful hydroponic gardening. So have the water analyzed. Your county agent will be happy to do it for you, or perhaps your water supply company or department can give you a complete analysis. A commercial agricultural or soil laboratory can also help you.

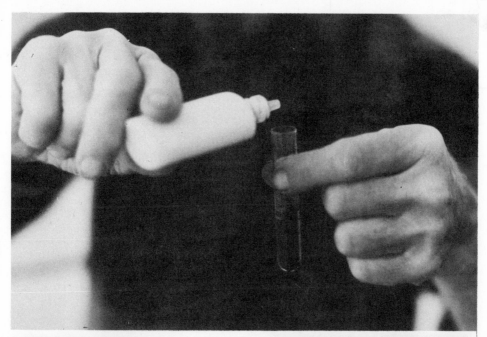

Another method utilizes a few drops of bromthymol blue in the nutrient solution, causing it to assume a shade of blue. This shade is then compared with those on a chart to get an approximate pH reading. Testing materials are available from garden supply shops.

It isn't expensive when you consider how your crop may turn out if you don't have it done!

With a good analysis in hand you are ready to move on to the consideration of nutrient solutions that will be the life of your food plants.

A typical water analysis report, obtainable from a commercial laboratory, or from your water supply company or agency.

WATER   ANALYSIS

	Milli equivalents per liter	Parts per million
TOTAL SOLIDS	---	887
DISSOLVED SOLIDS	---	823
SUSPENDED SOLIDS	---	64
pH		7.59
CONDUCTIVITY $ECx10^6$		1180
CARBONATES	none found	
BICARBONATES	6.5	397
CHLORIDES	4.2	149
SULFATES	1.0	48
NITRATES	0.3	20
CALCIUM	5.8	116
MAGNESIUM	0.3	4
SODIUM	5.9	136
% SODIUM (calculated)		49.2
BORON	trace	---
FLOURINE	0.4	0.4
TOTAL HARDNESS as $CaCO_3$ grains/gal.	17.5	299

Nutrient Solutions

Chapter 4

Nutrient Solutions:

balanced plant nutrition

So YOU WANT a lush, rapid, healthy growth of fruits and vegetables? In hydroponic gardening, as in any other kind, this depends most of all on a consistent supply of the right nutrients to the plant—at least 16 of them in all.

What does just one vital mineral withheld from the plant do to that plant? It stunts its growth in some way. Take cabbage, for example. Withhold calcium and more pitiful-looking cabbage you've never seen.

In ordinary gardening, even organic gardening, the soil may test well on the necessary nutrients, but some of them may be "locked," not actually available to the plant. Phosphate may be in such a form at times. So may

The nutrient solution in this home hydroponic greenhouse is contained in a waterproof concrete-lined tank below floor level. The solution is prepared by adding to the water a dry, soluble nutrient concentrate formulated by the supplier in relation to the water characteristics. A pump (lower right) feeds the solution twice a day into the growing trays (upper left). The solution then drains back into the tank by gravity flow (center) for continued reuse throughout the life of the solution (from 6-30 days). The solution is then pumped outside, fed by hose to yard plants, and is then replaced by fresh solution.

potassium, or iron, and others. To do the plant any good, all nutrients have to be present in a form usable by the plant.

Hydroponics Makes Nutrition Sure

This is one of the main advantages of hydroponic gardening. You can *always* be sure your plants have the necessary nutrients for vital, healthy growth and superior productivity.

How? Simply by putting those elements in the right form into the nutrient solution with which you irrigate the plants in their growing medium—that 7- or 9-inch-deep bed of gravel we spoke of earlier.

Essential Nutrients

Here are the nutrients known to be essential for optimum plant development:

Macronutrients	*Micronutrients or Trace Elements*
Carbon	Sodium
Nitrogen	Sulphur
Phosphorus	Iron
Potassium	Manganese
Calcium	Zinc
Magnesium	Copper
Hydrogen	Molybdenum
Oxygen	Boron
	Chlorine

In addition to the nutrients shown above, cobalt, iodine, and others may also become of greater interest as more is learned about the trace elements.

Generally, however, the salts in which the various nutrients are supplied are not in an absolutely pure state. Thus they usually contain trace elements in addition to those listed above.

Some nutrients are naturally in your water supply, such as sodium or chlorine, but not necessarily in the right proportion.

Some of the elements, such as carbon, hydrogen, and oxygen, the plant converts from water, from the air that reaches the roots during aeration, from other elements, and in other ways.

Nutrients "Fitted" to Your Water Supply

The nutrients not in your water supply, you must place there in careful balance, in amounts based on the existing characteristics of your water.

Various suppliers can provide concentrates with nutrients in the right proportion, if you give them a sample of your water or an analysis from your water company.

As you become more skilled in hydroponic gardening you can buy the nutrients individually and mix your own formulas. At first, however, you will probably want to buy them, prepared as dry mixtures to be added to your water to produce nutrient solution.

The nutrient solution will need to be tested, adjusted or replaced at regular intervals—four days, ten days, twenty days, depending on the needs of your particular plants and the specifications of the supplier.

Let's talk a bit about some of the individual nutrients. Sodium, for example, can serve as a replacement for potassium. But sodium also serves another key role in plant nutrition. Believe it or not, it makes a plant more drought resistant.

Chloride or chlorine, you will note, is one of the micronutrients.

Of the macronutrients, three are carbon, hydrogen, and oxygen. And you don't have to buy them. As we just mentioned, they are in air and water, and in combination with other elements. But you do have to add nitrogen or nitrates, phosphates, potassium, sulphur, calcium, and magnesium. You also have to add iron, zinc, manganese, boron, chlorine, molybdenum, and copper at least.

Now what part do they play? Well, let's talk about nitrogen or nitrates. About 85 percent of the air we breathe is nitrogen. But in what form can the plant take nitrogen? When it is a nitrate. Did you know that lightning helps to put nitrogen into nitrate form? It's available then, isn't it? Some plants can store nitrates and, plowed into the soil in regular farming, can benefit the crops that follow.

Nutrient Sources

What forms of nitrate can we get for hydroponic gardening? We can get ammonium nitrate, calcium nitrate, potassium nitrate, urea, diammonium phosphate. But, in whatever form, we know we need nitrate. And we can get it.

There are also many sources of phosphate and potassium. How are we going to get calcium? Remember, a lot of that may be in the water already. How are we going to get magnesium? A lot of that, too, may be in the water. Some trace elements are going to be there.

Nutrient Formulas

Any one of these will serve as your basic nutrient formula. The three given here vary only with respect to the availability of nutrients in various areas. Check with your garden or farm supplier. Use the quantities listed for each 10 gallons of water in your nutrient tank.

No. 1

1 oz. ammonium nitrate
1 oz. calcium sulfate
½ oz. magnesium sulfate
1 oz. potassium sulfate
½ oz. diammonium phosphate

No. 2

1 oz. sodium nitrate
1 oz. calcium nitrate
1 oz. potassium sulfate
½ oz. magnesium sulfate
1½ oz. single super phosphate

No. 3

1½ oz. potassium nitrate
2 oz. calcium nitrate
¾ oz. magnesium sulfate
½ oz. diammonium phosphate

Add water soluble trace elements to all of the above. Specify amounts for your water (see below). Any reliable soil or water analysis laboratory can help you locate these.

Don't forget the agriculture extension service of state universities for information on hydroponic solutions.

Trace Elements

The following fairly common and readily obtainable materials will supply the most important trace elements to your nutrient solution. However, you should still confer with your county agent to determine if the particular composition of your water supply suggests some adjustment in these amounts. You need both of these groups: they are combined this way because of their compatibility in these two concentrations.

GROUP ONE

½ tsp manganese chloride
1¼ tsp. boric acid powder
2 tsp. Fe330, iron chelate

Dissolve these materials in 1 gal. water; use 5 oz. of this concentrate for each 10 gal. of your nutrient solution.

GROUP TWO

1/2 tsp. zinc sulfate
1/5 tsp. copper sulfate

Dissolve these materials in 1 gal. of water; use 8 drops of this concentrate for each 10 gal. of nutrient solution.

But of all the minerals we put into our nutrient solution, how do we know what the plant actually takes up and uses? By tissue testing, and this can be done by your agricultural agent or a commercial laboratory.

Do you think a woman is fickle? Well, try testing plants. They are really fickle. You can set up a pattern of nutrient supply in October under a given mean temperature for the climate in that year, and you may find the plants really taking up the potassium, for example. Check them the next year under apparently the same conditions, at the same time, and they may not be taking so much of it.

Plants "Select" Nutrients from Balanced Solution

So what is the important thing? That you have balanced nutrition, balanced nutrient solutions. Every time we pump the solution to the plant roots in those gravel beds, we are going to present a balanced solution. Then, whatever the conditions, the plant is going to take what it needs, as it "feels" it needs it. Many factors affect the uptake of nutrients. Lots of things. But man can't decide what the plant is going to take. He can only present a balanced nutrient solution to the plant and let nature make the final nutritional decisions.

Now the plant has to have all these nutrients available all the time. Let me tell you what happens if there is a lack of potassium, for example. Have you ever had mulberry trees develop that little crinkle-crisp edge on the leaf, and wonder why? You possibly called out an expert and he said, "Well, you have a sodium burn

Two-year-old Anne Sturtevant looks over the beautiful, deep-green cabbage plants in her parents' hydroponic garden. Healthy food plants do help to make healthy children.

there." Then perhaps another expert looked at it and said, "You have a lack of potassium." Which one was right? They were both right. If the potassium isn't there, the plant is going to take sodium in its place and you may get a "sodium burn."

So in making nutrients available to the plant, we must make sure that we always have an adequate level of potassium, particularly if sodium is naturally in the water.

Consider molybdenum—one of the micronutrients or trace elements. The need for it is so minute—.02 parts per million—that it is a bit dangerous to add it to the solution. So if a molybdenum deficiency shows up, such as leaf mottling, don't get excited and rashly add too much molybdenum. In all probability the other minerals in your nutrient solution will carry, as "impurities," enough molybdenum to serve the need. Even if the "impurities" don't include enough molybdenum, a wonderful thing takes place. The plant will utilize the ionic structure of nitrates to take care of that deficiency. It is amazing what powers of chemistry the Creator has placed in plant life.

No Worries About Overfertilizing

Can you oversupply a plant with nutrients? No, not in a balanced form. Have you ever "burned" anything with fertilizer? Well, what happened in that case? The plant epidermis, or the root epidermis, has an osmotic membrane. In osmosis, as you know, water moves from one area to another, through a membrane.

A fertilizer burn results from too much salts, too high a concentration of salts, in the water solution next to the root in the soil. When the water supply is limited, the salts become too concentrated, and the salts actually take the moisture from the inside of that root membrane. The plant dries up and dies.

Let's talk more about sodium. In some areas, one of the main things people ask me for help on is dichondra lawns. They spend all kinds of money and effort and all they have for their expense and trouble is a thin, yellow patch of dichondra. Do you know what my advice often is? I tell them to put detergent on that dichondra! I hope no ecologists are going to scold me for that! The villain is sodium in the ground, and it is tying up many nutrients. It is trying to replace potassium, for example. Furthermore, it's causing chlorosis, or an iron deficiency, even when there is plenty of iron in the soil.

Wetting Agents

Now what happens when we add a detergent? Years ago I was working on a small public park in Cushing, Oklahoma. A representative of an oil drilling company came to see me there with some cages full of the most pitiful creatures you've ever seen. I thought at first he had something pretty dangerous in those cages. Actually, it turned out to be a lot of very oily ducks! The man said those ducks had landed on the slush pit the night before, apparently thinking it was a beautiful lagoon. Instead of a little rest, they got a lot of sticky oil and much frustration. The man didn't want to kill them so here he was, presenting them to me to clean up—about a hundred of the poor sticky things.

Well, in the park there was a little lagoon that already had a lot of ducks on it. We took the unfortunate ones down there and started washing them in detergent. And will that ever clean up a duck! Man, they just feel like something brand new. What are you going to do with a duck after you get him cleaned up? You're going to throw him out there in the water, aren't you? That's what we did, all right—and they sank like rocks! Down they went. And there I was, in 28° weather in Cushing, Oklahoma, fully clad in work clothes, trying to keep ducks from sinking!

We finally rescued them all, nearly needing to be

rescued ourselves in the process. We took the ducks to a barn and kept them there until their natural oil returned. You know what happened, don't you? Detergent is a super-wetting agent that breaks the surface tension of water. The water, normally repelled by the oil in the ducks' plumage, penetrated the plumage instead and their natural "life jacket" was gone.

In a similar way, detergent as a wetting agent helps nutrients to penetrate the soil and do some good. Do you know what a cocculus laurafolius is? It's a long, big-leaf thing that some call a laurel leaf. We had one of those at our house that just decided it was going to be a midget. It was never going to grow. It was right there by the front door, and I didn't know what to do with it. My wife, in desperation, gave it some detergent. She really endangered the mailman's life because that thing started growing and it was grabbing for the sun and everything else it could reach.

Then, there was a chain of markets wanting me to grow bougainvillaea to be sold in bloom at a time of year when the plants wouldn't normally be in bloom. I was trying to bring on 2,000 of these things and I couldn't get them to bloom. Wham! I gave them the detergent and color started spilling out all over the place. Those things were in such a state of brilliant shock I couldn't believe it. My wife said, "What went on there?"

Nutrient Availability Is Vital

What *was* happening there? You know by now what's in detergent, don't you? It contains phosphate, nitrate, potassium, and many other goodies. More than that, its function as a wetting agent helps the nutrients to get to the plants, in solution and usable.

In one of my operations one time, we were turning out about 5,000 tons of compost a month. A lady called after everybody else had gone home one evening and wanted a load of that compost. I took it out to her place and she said, "Since you're here anyway and since you have your shovel, I don't suppose you would charge me anything to put that around my roses." I put it on for her. I still remember trying to explain to my wife why I didn't get home for dinner until eight o'clock.

I had picked that woman out as being a super grouch. In a couple of weeks she called me, sounding as if she were in a rage. (I'm apprehensive about dealing with women, anyway.) She told me to come out to her house. Bang! The phone went dead.

Well, I went out to her house. She said, "I want you to see my roses." I had seen them from my truck but it didn't seem to me that anything was wrong with them. She startled me by saying, "My husband will put $50,000 into your business if you will tell us what your secret fertilizer is in that compost." Oh, there would be one-half percent nitrate, maybe one and one-half percent of phosphate, possibly some potassium, etc.

But what improved her roses so much? You put mulch on top of something and water in the soil percolates, doesn't it? You put it on, it goes down and then it tries to come back up. What stops it? The mulch. And roses love to be mulched. The microbial activity is increased. Earthworms can work better. The soil becomes more friable and more oxygen can work under this mulch.

So what had we done? Simply this: We had *activated*

the nutrient solution. We had put all the nutrients into solution. So remember this: While we've been discussing ducks, detergent, compost, and things growing better, we have been talking about *nutrients in solution.*

Hydroponics Solves Many Problems

This is the beauty of hydroponics. We don't have to worry about compacted soil blocking nutrients from the plants. We know our nutrients are the right ones, in usable form, and we know they will get to plants. We know that, because we have pumps pumping the nutrients into the growing trays twice a day. Then the nutrient drains back into the storage tanks and the gravel growing medium in the trays is aerated.

We don't have the compaction problems. We don't get the water just once a week or once a month. We didn't inherit a bunch of sodium in the ground, did we? We have a completely clean gravel growing medium. We don't have percolation and evaporation bringing up and depositing salt at the surface of our growing medium as they do in some kinds of soil.

These things are not problems in hydroponics. Because everything is growing in a clean, aerated medium and being fed a balanced, controlled nutrient solution. The nutrient solution goes in, the nutrient solution goes out—twice a day. What is left in the gravel after the solution goes out? Capillary moisture—on the surface of every piece of gravel. And there's where the nutrients are. Are they too strong for your plant? No. We used to figure that if we had too much nitrate in the soil, it would inhibit the germination of seed. That was correct.

But we know that we can be watering with hydroponic nutrient solutions and drop seeds right in the gravel, even while that solution is going through, and those seeds will germinate.

Good Balance Better Than "Tinkering"

When I mentioned the 16 elements needed for plant nutrition, I included sodium. Even though it is often not considered a "required" element, why did I mention it? Because it serves as a catalyst in the plant's uptake of potassium. Moreover, in many parts of the country, sodium can be a villain if sufficient potassium is not present. So we do want to be sure that adequate potassium is in the nutrient solution so that its absence is not a limiting factor in plant growth. Remember that the plant will take sodium if potassium is not there; and although the plant will take sodium, it's not going to be helped by it alone. It still needs the potassium.

Sometimes when I list the nutrients, someone says molybdenum is not a micronutrient. It is and it isn't. It depends on which book you're reading. But it is something with which we have to reckon. Remember that you can develop toxicities in plants in any kind of agriculture if you put in too much of the wrong trace element. You can get toxicities in cattle feed, for example, if there's too much nitrate. There can also be zinc toxicities in plants if you're not careful. The same care is necessary in hydroponics as in conventional gardening.

If you are keeping your nutrient solution balanced and you test it at regular intervals; then, further, if you test the plants to see what they are taking up, you are practicing good gardening.

I mentioned the routine: a pH check every four days, and a nutrient check at intervals recommended by the supplier of your nutrient powders. Nitrates, for example, should be checked every 10 days. In fact, 10 days isn't a bad interval for checking all the nutrients, generally speaking.

Renew, Don't Manipulate Solution

But let me tell you a personal secret. I don't actually test and "doctor" or manipulate my nutrient solutions. A complete analysis takes a lot of time or perhaps a fee of $20 to a laboratory. It is less costly for me to have my solutions formulated to contain the nutrients they will need for, say, five days or ten days or for whatever period I'm going to use it. Then at the end of that time, I pump that solution out onto trees or other things around my place that are being neglected anyway—and refill my tanks with fresh solution.

However, there are different times of the year in which you'll find that the nitrate needs to be built up, for example; or the phosphate or the potassium. Testing of the solution will tell you this, or testing the plants; or more likely, your increasing experience in noting signs of various deficiencies in the appearance of the plants.

In places where water is precious and costly, it pays to test and adjust the solutions. In hydroponic gardening in the Middle East, for example, they can keep that water going—testing and adding, testing and adding, for at least three months. In that case you would want some pretty accurate testing, wouldn't you?

I helped to set up a commercial hydroponics unit at a

Nutrients come in powder or granular form. They can be carefully mixed in correct proportion by the home gardener—adapted to his water supply—or purchased ready-formulated from various suppliers.

NUTRIENTS IN SOLUTION
Range of Tolerance for Most Plants

	MIN.	MAX.		MIN.	MAX.
Nitrate	200	1000	Iron	0.5-2	—
Ammonium	—	100	Boric acid	0.2-1	5
Phosphorus	30	100	Zinc	0.2-2	20
Potassium	150	600	Copper	0.1-2	5
Magnesium	25	150	Manganese	1-5	15
Sulfate	150	1000	Cobalt		
Chloride	30	600	Fluoride		
Sodium	—	400	Molybdenum		

All amounts in parts per million

county fair in southern California to run about 20 days on a single filling of nutrient solution, and the plants were fabulous. No one was ever there. The greenhouse was locked up and it just ran automatically.

Actually, I admonish people running a hydroponic unit to visit it every day, even if it is automatc. If you don't do some work in it, just say hello to the plants!

One reason I could mix a 20-day solution for that greenhouse is that it contained a variety of vegetables. The solution "life" depends on what we're growing. With squash alone, for example, I could run a nutrient solution 30 days without testing.

The pH Requires Adjustment

The pH is the most critical and regular thing to test once your nutrient solution is established. You keep the pH at a constant 6.5 if you can. But let me tell you something about pH. Starting with a 7.8 pH and dropping it to 6.5 takes 16 ounces of concentrated sulphuric acid (66° BE) for 1,050 gallons. Now I have a pH of 6.5. But what happens when I put in the nitrate? The pH goes back up again. It is buffered. So I test again for the pH, still trying to keep it in the 6.5 range. Maybe I drop it down to 6.0. Maybe I push it up to 7.0. My target is 6.5, with a tolerance of half a point either way.

The Growing Medium

Chapter 5

The Growing Medium:

disease-free "soil"

WHAT HOLDS THE plant and its root structure securely
—in hydroponic gardening? The growing medium. Its
basic function is as simple as you can imagine—just
holding the plant up so it can flourish while you nourish
it twice a day with your nutrient solution.

But still, that growing medium has to have certain
characteristics if it is going to do its best for you. Let me
tell you what those are in just a minute, then you can
see why I prefer just plain, clean gravel, with the piece
size about three-eighths of an inch. Of course, when I say
clean, I mean sterile, with no disease-producing organisms—and I'll tell you about that in another chapter.

You may be amazed at some of the things that could be and are, in fact, used as growing media in hydroponic gardening: straw, wood chips, sawdust, peat moss, sand, crushed brick, perlite, vermiculite, glass marbles, sponge rubber, plastic foam scraps, broken dishes—broken records!

Straw is an interesting medium. You know, it is self-sterilizing. If you get a bale of straw wet, the center temperature will go how high? About 160 degrees. And that will sterilize it of anything harmful to your plants. You can plant something right in that straw and water it with a nutrient solution.

Of course, once you get it hot, you need to cool it off. It takes only about 48 hours to bring up the center heat. And you can check that with a thermometer. When it gets hot, just start putting the water to it before it breaks down. If you don't, that bale of straw will just turn to "ashes," won't it?

Straw also has another quality we need in our growing medium—porosity. It will absorb and hold the nutrient solution long enough for the plant to utilize it.

But remember something about straw. It has what we call high-carbon tissue. Lots of nitrogen is needed to help that carbon disintegrate. So to the nutrient solution we would have to add lots of nitrogen.

Let's talk briefly about another type of growing medium. Do you like sprouted alfalfa seed? It sprouts very well on nothing more than sponge rubber or plastic foam. Just lay the seeds on top and moisten the material occasionally. There is no need to cover it, although it may be useful to have the material in a pan or similar container. The seeds will sprout very nicely. So will

An amazing variety of growing media can serve in hydroponic gardening even though gravel is considered best. Lush cauliflower is shown here, grown in a sand and sawdust mixture by Dr. and Mrs. D. L. Stoops. Nutrient solution is poured directly onto the mixture at regular intervals. The growing tray is lined with polyethelene plastic.

chia seeds; some people like those. I use foam plastic for testing the germination of various seed. It could, in fact, be used as a growing medium for a number of plant types.

We could say a great deal about many kinds of growing media, but the main reason I mentioned such a variety was to help you to realize that it isn't necessary

to have plants growing in soil, as such, in order to have
healthy, flourishing plants.

Function of Growing Medium

The function of soil is to provide a growing medium
—something for root and plant support, and nutrients.
In hydroponic gardening we accomplish this in different
ways, ways that enable us to control the plants' total
environment—for optimum growth and nutrition and
minimum hazards from pests and disease.

In considering the best plant growing media we need
to remember that we are going to work in a fairly small
area. What, then, is the easiest medium in which to
work?

Look at some of the problems. When we take out an
old plant we don't want to leave a lot of root debris in
the medium. It will just rot. So we want a medium from
which we can easily recover the roots. If I have planted
in peat moss and I want to pull out a plant, what will
I have along with the roots? A big hunk of peat moss.
Then I can sit there and be a peat moss picker or I can
buy some more peat moss.

If I have been growing my plants in sand, what happens? They are easily recovered but the roots will shear
off if the sand is too wet and heavy when I pull out the
plant.

But what if my plants are in gravel? How well can I
recover the roots? Almost completely.

Another question to consider in selecting a plant
growing medium: how easy is it to sterilize? Straw is
easy to sterilize, but when it starts to break down it can

Particles of red lava are the growing medium for this prize cocozelle squash, planted in a plastic utility tub. The plant is fed regularly with nutrient solution, with the roots allowed to aerate well between feedings.

also bring many fungus invasions. Straw can be a host to many kinds of fungus and mildew.

Of course, not all fungus and mildew are harmful. Some are friendly. But to me a snake is a snake until I get a better look at it. Neither do you know which is good and which is bad fungus, or which is good and which is bad mildew on sight. And you certainly don't have time to have a lab culture run on it. So I wouldn't use straw unless I had to, and then only in an open air situation; not in a greenhouse.

In hydroponics we want a controlled environment, and the growing medium must help us to control the

On most counts, gravel is the preferred growing medium for hydroponic gardening. It is stable; does not alter the nutrient solution; holds roots firmly, yet old roots are easily pulled from it to make room for new plants.

environment—not add to our problems. For example, in our greenhouses the humidity is usually high, so we want a growing medium that will easily aerate. We want something that can easily be fumigated. If we should ever have to use a fungicide we want a medium that has a high porosity so that the fungicide will go through and coat every place in the medium where there is moisture. Gravel has the characteristics that enable us to do these things.

Another reason I use gravel as a growing medium is because it does not absorb and hold heat from the sun as some people think it does. Perlite, for example, in a lot of sunlight, can actually give plants a reflective scorch.

Now why should I prefer gravel over sand? Because in sand I'm going to get some flocculation, with some nutrients like calcium or magnesium collecting into clumps in the sand. I'm not going to get that in gravel.

Gravel is easily changed, when necessary. It's heavy to shovel, I'll admit that. But if you ever do have to change the gravel in a growing tray, you can shovel all of it out. Any remainder you can sweep up with a broom. You can get it all out. There is not a lot of scrubbing down to do. You won't have to clean up mildew or other organisms as you do with vermiculite or soils or peat mosses or that sort of thing.

Gravel is Dependable

Gravel is a very dependable medium. It is a medium that will stay classified. If we use sand and have to add sawdust to it, the sawdust does rot away and thus the medium changes. Now this is not a big problem between crops, but it is a problem on some kinds of crops. Also, sand will sometimes tighten up. But we know that when we put solutions into gravel, every part of that growing medium is getting the same amount of moisture and nutrients.

We know that when we drain away the nutrient solution, there will be good aeration of the plant root structure. We know that various nutrients will not tend to flocculate, or collect in various places and possibly injure the plants.

We know that in every possible way the growing medium is helping us to control the environment and produce a uniformly high quality product.

Now, what do we use to contain the growing medium, what kind of container? What system do we use to get the nutrient solution into that growing medium and drain it away again? What kinds of greenhouse structures can we use within which we can create and maintain the ideal environment for our plants? That's what the next chapter is all about.

The Hydroponic Greenhouse

Chapter 6

The Hydroponic Greenhouse:

a controlled environment

YOU DON'T NEED a greenhouse in order to grow plants hydroponically. The basic principal, feeding the plants with nutrient solutions, can be applied in many ways.

For example, on the ultrasimple side, you can fill a plastic dishpan half-full of gravel, drill a hole in the bottom and stop it up with a cork. Put your plants in the gravel and water them twice a day by pouring a bucketful of nutrient solution in the dishpan. After 15 minutes or so, pull the plug and let the solution drain out of the pan back into the bucket, ready for use again. Do that just twice a day. Be sure your plants get plenty of light and don't suffer from extreme temperatures—

Hydroponics can be practiced in many forms. Here is a window tray (fiberglass), filled nearly to the top with gravel. The nutrient solution is contained in the plastic pail (left), which is connected to the tray by a plastic hose. Twice a day the pail is placed on a higher stool to let the solution drain into the tray, then lowered to let it drain back into the pail. How does your garden grow? Easily!

and you have a hydroponic garden going! You saw some earlier in the book—and above—to prove it.

You can do the same thing with sand and sawdust or any of the other growing media we discussed in the last chapter. You don't even have to have it set up so you can reuse your nutrient solution if you don't want to. Put your plants into a growing medium in an ordinary flower pot and just feed them the nutrient solution at regular intervals, being sure the medium allows ample aeration of the roots between feedings.

However—and that's a big however—you won't realize the real pleasure, the real convenience, the real productivity, of modern hydroponics without some kind of greenhouse.

Here you can install relatively inexpensive automatic controls in order to maintain, with minimum effort, the optimum environment for your plants.

Pumps, actuated by a timeclock, can feed the nutrient solution to your plants in their growing trays, then let the solution drain back into the tank for recycling later in the day.

Heaters and coolers can automatically maintain temperature and humidity within the best growing range.

Your work is to get the plants started, fill your tank with nutrient solution, let the automatic equipment do the rest while you have the pleasure of training your vines or other plants as they grow upward on strings or stakes to take full advantage of your space—just enjoy watching them grow, and pluck the harvest!

You do have to check your nutrient solution regularly to be sure the pH of the water is in a safe range; keep the water level in the nutrient solution tank up to at least 90 percent of the original amount (even this can be automated with a float valve); and be on the alert to keep admiring neighbors from bringing disease organisms into your controlled environment.

The nutrient solution in the tank needs to be changed at whatever interval it has been formulated for—usually about once a week.

But all this adds up to only about 15 to 20 minutes a day of essential work—and as many hours a day of pleasure as you care to enjoy.

So, you see—hydroponic gardening can be as simple or as elaborate as you wish.

Greenhouses—Simple or Elaborate

Even a greenhouse can be a simple, inexpensive structure made of two-by-fours and plastic sheeting; it can be a somewhat more elaborate do-it-yourself building; or it can be one of the professionally designed hydroponic greenhouse "packages" offered by various manufacturers—most of whom also offer installation and consulting services.

One of the author's friends, James Hallsted, chose to build this attractive, yet relatively simple greenhouse. Inexpensive, but effective. It is not fully automated and involves a bit more time, but still produces lush, hydroponic crops.

Bill Haas talks with the author about his hydroponic greenhouse, a splendid example of what the home gardener can produce when he goes all-out to make it the very best. This greenhouse is a fully-automated, year-round "food factory."

Whether you buy or build, your greenhouse has to be suited to the area you live in and its environmental characteristics—to say nothing of the size you can put into your backyard! You may want one 12 feet by 12 feet, or one 24 feet by 40 feet.

Actually a greenhouse only 10 feet by 12 feet, with efficient arrangement of the plants, can provide all the fresh produce needed by a family of four or five.

Greenhouses vs. Deep Freeze

And remember this, cubic foot for cubic foot a greenhouse costs a lot less than a freezer and will contain a lot more food! Had you rather get your food fresh every day from your greenhouse or frozen from the freezer? Me, too! I'll take mine fresh.

Let's talk about greenhouse construction.

Some years ago, I helped a man build a greenhouse in southern California. We tried to find out what kind of wind we were going to have in that particular spot. "Well, it gets pretty windy," some oldtimers said.

How windy? We measured the wind one day. Eighty-five miles an hour! That kind of wind didn't come very often, but what was it going to blow away when it did come? Everything that couldn't withstand an 85-mile-an-hour wind. So what kind of a greenhouse would you build there? One with specifications that would stand a 25-mile-an-hour wind?

No. Because, I'll tell you, the components of a greenhouse are easier to put together the first time than when you take them up, a twisted ruin, and try to put them back together. So build a greenhouse to specifications appropriate to your area.

One major question in greenhouse construction is pretty elementary: where are we going to put it? What is a good location? Where you have some sunlight. What else? Not where you have a lot of small vandals, or other kinds of pests that may attack it. You don't want that location. Protection from the wind is a consideration.

How about where the zoning man told you not to build it? That's not such a good place, is it? How about where some development promoter said, "Well, the flood's never going to come through here again. Why should we build houses here if water were ever going to come through here again?" Sure. Has that ever happened around where you live?

If you live close to a coastline where it's foggy most of the time you need to consider heating problems. If you are out on the desert where the sun shines all the time, then cooling will be more of a consideration.

If you are near a big body of water, an inland lake— that's great, because it helps to moderate the temperature changes.

We need to consider the availability of utilities, don't we? We need natural gas, if possible. We need water. We need electricity.

What can I use for heat if I don't have natural gas? Anything that will burn that's economical. Butane, propane—sawdust, if you want. I don't care, because what can we use in a greenhouse for heat? We can use forced air, can't we? Air circulated in the greenhouse from a heating mechanism outside the greenhouse, if necessary. We can use steam. Can we use copper lines with hot water in the floor of the greenhouse? Yes. Anything to keep that greenhouse warm, economically.

A controlled climate for maximum food production. Bill Haas demonstrates temperature controls. Note also the exhaust fan and free-swinging louvers. There is also an evaporative cooler and a heater, both controlled automatically.

What about lighting in the greenhouse? Are we going to hang electric lights all over the greenhouse? I don't think so, because it's not going to pay off. There again it's a question of economics. But we do want adequate light.

What kind of water do we need? In hydroponics, we can get by with almost any kind of water, can't we? Can we use salt water? Yes. But we won't get the crop production that we would get from good water. Our rule is: get everything in our favor we can get so we don't have too many surprises. Right? So let's get the best heating, the best cooling, the best water, the best location.

Equipment for Good Housekeeping

One of the major factors in greenhouse gardening is housekeeping. You do want to keep the place clean. Therefore, you want your greenhouse built so it is easy to keep clean. That has a lot to do with the kind and the physical arrangement of the equipment in that house.

Consider the air-moving, air-cooling equipment, for example. This is going to have quite an effect in keeping down fungus, mildew, and bacterial problems. A greenhouse needs at least one air change per minute when you are operating evaporative cooling systems; and, in some greenhouses, an evaporative cooler is quite adequate. In a larger, commercial greenhouse, in fact, one whole end of the greenhouse may be an evaporative cooling pad with exhaust fans at the other end of the house to pull the air through.

In a small greenhouse the cooler may be what some

call the little swamp cooler. It's desirable in two ways. One, it will cool your greenhouse when the weather is hot. Two, when the humidity is low, it will provide humidity.

Even if you don't have a cooling or a humidity problem, you still have to change the air or at least have it circulating in the greenhouse. I prefer continuous air circulation in a greenhouse—24 hours a day—and I will tell you why. The plant has quite a cooling mechanism

The author checks a student's luxuriant green bean growth in a more simple greenhouse. Note the nutrient solutions, in containers (lower right), applied by hand to the gravel in the growing tray rather than being automatically pumped and recycled. Note also the free-swinging louvers for air pressure equalization (top) and the simple fan for air circulation. Note also an ordinary evaporative cooler (lower right) for humidity and temperature control.

of its own, doesn't it? It is one of the effects of transpiration. This pulls the nutrients, the water, up through the plant and keeps it functioning well. The transpiration rate means the rate at which the moisture comes out of the leaves. If you are moving air all of the time, and the plant is transpiring all of the time, you do not have the fungus, mildew, and bacterial problems that you would have if your air were not moving.

So, is the air-control system part of the housekeeping in your greenhouse? It certainly is.

Incidentally, the air system should not be just a fan, moving air around inside a sealed greenhouse. You need some carbon dioxide in the daytime and you need some oxygen at night. Also, if you build a greenhouse too tight, and leave it too tight, what happens to the flame in your heater? It will burn up the oxygen, and go out.

I once had to help a friend who had built a shelter to protect his plants on a freezing night. He sealed in the whole area with polyethylene plastic. He had left a few leaks, but they weren't sufficient. Apparently the flame had gone out sometime before he got there about six o'clock the next morning. As he opened the door, he lit a cigarette. He was lucky he was wearing a heavy horsehide jacket, because that is what burned instead of him! He managed to get rid of it in time. We don't build greenhouses so tight that some air can't get in.

If you have some free-swinging louvers at the end of a greenhouse, they are a big help, especially in equalizing air pressure in the greenhouse during a storm.

When we are ready for greenhouse design and construction, where can we go for help? There again, you

A miniature watermelon vine reaches for the top of the greenhouse. Note the louver in the end of the greenhouse for air circulation and air pressure equalization.

pay taxes for it. Cash in on it. Check with your county agricultural agent, the extension division of state universities' agricultural departments, or the United States Department of Agriculture.

If you are going to buy a greenhouse, check out the people you are buying it from to be sure they have a good reputation and will build you an operable greenhouse. Go see the kind of house they are going to sell you. If you are dealing with a good company, chances are you will get more for your money than by building the same thing yourself.

I know a man who had an opportunity to buy a greenhouse for about $1,500. He was quite a clever man and decided he would save money and do it himself. He did a good job of building, and it cost him only $2,000! Now, he finds, there are a lot of things about it he doesn't like; that he'd like to change. There are indeed mistakes that we can make when we build our own greenhouses.

Greenhouse Covering

What about the covering of a greenhouse? The frame can be wood, steel pipe, or what have you, but the cover is what protects your plants and lets in the life-giving light. That cover has to be strong enough to withstand the wind. You don't want it to melt in the rain. You want the cover to let the light in. You want the cover to keep the cold out. You want it to be pretty durable. But you don't want it to be the major cost of the greenhouse.

Among the materials you can use is polyethylene

Probably the best and most durable greenhouse covering is corrugated Filon, shown here by Bill Haas. Note that this west-facing side of greenhouse is white-washed for reduction of heat and radiation from afternoon sun, a problem in Mr. Haas' area.

plastic. You can also use PVC plastic roll sheeting; polyvinyl chloride, hence the PVC abbreviation.

You can use Filon. That's a corrugated fiberglass sheeting of good quality. It is semi-clear and should give you sufficient light for at least ten years.

For some of these materials you will need to go to a manufacturer whose products require him to stock them, because they are sold from the factory only in very large quantities. Most manufacturers will sell you some. You will pay a little profit, but that's a lot cheaper than your inventory would be if you had to buy what the factory required.

Now, if you are inclined toward interior and exterior decorating, forget having a pretty little greenhouse with green Filon or orange Filon, or red Filon. Okay? The lumber and building supply man may try to help you because he sells that type of Filon. But it is not semi-clear Filon. Remember, you're not buying this to look pretty, necessarily. You are buying it so that your vegetables will be pretty. And there's nothing prettier than a verdant green vegetable or a green tomato vine with a red fruit hanging on it. Those colors are good enough for anyone. What you want in the greenhouse covering itself is light transmission.

In colder climates, I recommend a two-layer covering. I would make the inside layer of PVC sheeting and the outside layer of Filon, the two layers about two to four inches apart. In addition to light transmission you will have better insulation between two dissimilar materials.

This double thickness with four inches of dead space between will change the temperature by eleven degrees. You save the cost, really, in lower heating requirements.

Also, in hot weather, you save some on cooling. But, except in extreme climates, the cost may be excessive in relation to benefit.

Quality Is Economical

How much greenhouse can you afford?

That's a pretty good question. How much car can you afford?

Some people can afford Cadillacs. For them, Cadillacs save money. Some of us have to be happy with whatever we can get, and we are. But seriously, what are you going to use this greenhouse for? You are using it for your family's health and well-being, aren't you? If the basic cost is getting up to around $1,500; or perhaps if you are really elaborate, $3,000 or even $5,000; and you save $100 by some economizing that makes the difference between the system working and not working, what have you really saved? Nothing.

This has to do with the quality of timeclocks. This has to do with pumps. This has to do with paint. This has to do with the whole system. Buy the best you can. Buy it from someone who can guarantee it and make the guarantee good.

Greenhouse "Packages"

If you do buy a greenhouse, approximately how much are you going to pay? It depends on the size and equipment. Let's start with size. You can buy very good ones for $1,595, 10 feet by 12. I can't see you having any problem with them for four or five years. Then you may only have to replace a cooler. But I think you would have to replace any cooler in about that length of time. I know their growing trays aren't going to leak or things like that.

In general, hydroponic greenhouse "packages" that cost only $7 a foot are a real bargain, assuming good quality. Such a package should include the pump, timers, coolers—everything, with the planting instructions and a six-month supply of nutrient. And, of course, most of these reputable companies have their own consultation service.

Various firms market complete hydroponic greenhouse "packages." Such packages typically include framing and covering materials, growing trays, cooler, heater, controls, nutrient solution tank, pump, a supply of nutrient solutions, and instructions. In some cases, the firms also maintain a continuing advisory service.

Now, remember, you don't have to buy a commercially-marketed greenhouse in order to do hydroponic growing. You can build just a growing tray and put it by a window if you want to.

But also remember, cubic foot for cubic foot a greenhouse is cheaper than a deep freeze; and a whole lot better for you.

"Therapy" in the Greenhouse

Until you try it, you can't believe the therapeutic value of a greenhouse—far beyond the value of the nutritious food it produces. Many of you have some tensions, don't you? I certainly do. I sneak off to the greenhouse and it does a lot for me. I've told you that plants are living things. They are appreciative living things.

I almost went to jail for murder one time. I was going with a girl and I thought she was pretty great. But apparently I didn't realize how great she thought she was. I bought her a very expensive gift and she scolded me because she thought it was too cheap! I was just that far from being in jail for murder. Not only would I have admitted it; I would have boasted about it!

But when I am around growing, living, appreciative things, I am relaxed. I'm not a cattle man, but not far from my greenhouse there are some fine black Angus. I like to stop by and scratch their heads. They appreciate it. They don't tell me the last fellow who was over scratched their heads better.

Do I talk to my plants? Yes, I'm happy I talk to my plants. It helps me, at least, and I am enough of a sentimentalist to think it helps them.

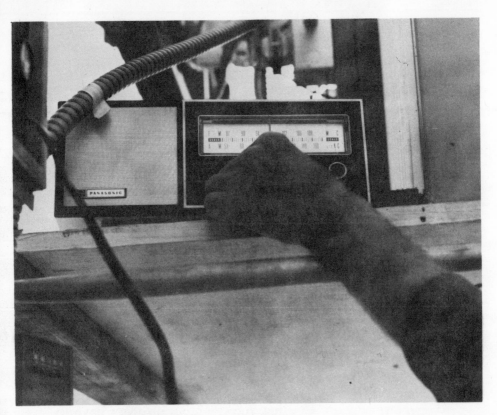

Talk to the plants? Sure. The author does! Other people play music to them—how about this FM radio as "greenhouse equipment"!

So why would you want a greenhouse? It will put you in touch with the Creator in a way that is hard to describe, because you see what He is doing for you. When you go in there and see how He has designed the mechanism of those plants and you watch them grow, you are really in touch with life. You can take your children or your grandchildren in there and show them these things.

Greenhouse Protection

Of course, children can also be one of the "pests" you may need to protect your plants from. And some mothers don't seem to teach them any better. Those

mothers get up at six o'clock in the morning and get
those darling little things out of bed, push them out of
the house, and lock the door on them. Then the kids
start tearing up everything that's pretty.

An Italian woman in my neighborhood came by one
day as I was repairing some damage done by the cute
little people. She could see I was distraught. "You take
all of the little children into your garden," she suggested; "and you have them pick flowers to take to their
mothers. From then on, you will have a built-in protection system.

Well I did. The little children came in, picked
flowers, and took them to their mothers. I told them
you shouldn't pick a flower unless you're going to take
it to your mother. You know what? I had a good protection system.

Now why am I telling you this? Because you have to
have this "protection system" when you build a greenhouse. Not always because of the little people, but
because of their mothers.

Finally I got those mothers to where *they* were coming out at six in the morning when I was picking flowers.
You know that when you are growing flowers—
whether you sell them or give them away or whatever
you do—you have to pick them every day. Did you
know that? Or you're going to be out of production.

I wish I had been a photographer in those days and
had pictures of these sleepy-eyed women with their robes
on, with their hair uncombed, standing there with a
bucket or basket waiting for me to fill it up with
flowers; then waking them up and saying, "You can go
home now, Mrs. Gordon. You've got your flowers."

And they would drag on home. But do you know what? Whenever I visited their homes—man, I had an iced tea, lemonade, lemon pie route beyond belief! When I went to the store, people I had given flowers to were inviting me in. I got the royal treatment. I don't care who they were. I got the very best. These were people who had flowers on the table from my greenhouse. I didn't think much of it in those days. I realize now what a lavish world I was living in!

Of course, hydroponics can be used for outdoor growing, too; particularly in the summer for things that need lots of room. But basically I want you to grow your plants—food or flowers—in a greenhouse. Why? Because in a greenhouse, gardening can be truly automated.

You will keep disease and pests away. No poodles or other pets will ruin your work. No wind will blow in weed seed. No insect invasions, and your plants get consistent water and nutrients in a clean, consistent atmosphere.

Growing Trays

Now let's look at that part of the greenhouse at which you will be spending most of those enjoyable hours with your plants—the growing trays.

These are the trays for the three-eighths-inch gravel (remember—our preferred growing medium) in which you place your seed or plants; and through which twice a day you will run the nutrient solution—whether by hand or by an automated pumping system.

Trays can take many forms in hydroponics—whatever

Growing trays may be made from many kinds of materials (see text). Boards lined with plastic; formed concrete lined with boards that are lined, in turn, with plastic (above); or pre-formed fiberglass (commonly supplied with greenhouse packages). They may be at floor level or placed on benches for easier access to smaller plants. Climbing vines and plants are tied to strings attached to an overhead wire for maximum use of vertical space.

is most economical in a given area to satisfactorily per-
form the function. And that function is simple—to
contain the growing medium and the nutrient solution
without leakage.

In India where they have a lot of clay, they tamp the
clay, then line it with asphalt. In Israel they often use
concrete beds coated with a bituminous material. In
Tanzania, where they don't have a lot of wood, they
build a 25- by 5-foot tray of concrete for only $2.40
worth of material.

You can make a growing tray from wood—six to
eight inches deep and, say, two or three feet wide; long
enough to use your space efficiently and still walk
around it.

Back in the 1930's some of the first hydroponic trays
I saw were made just that way and from pretty coarse,
rough lumber at that. They put a little caulking in the
cracks to prevent leakage. But some of them were made
of cypress—which leaks for a while, swells up and seals
itself.

But wooden trays should generally be lined with
plastic or rubber sheeting or asphalt in order to conserve
the nutrient solution.

Of course, wood is going to rot sooner or later; that's
why we don't use it much any more. Today, it is convenient and relatively inexpensive to get preformed
trays of fiberglass or asbestos. In fact, most of the
commercial hydroponic "packages" come with this kind
of tray; they are almost indestructible.

In some trays, the bottom slopes from either side to
the center, making a channel for the return of the
nutrient solution. Often a perforated pipe or hose is laid

in this channel. The solution is pumped out of the tank into this pipe and the solution rises in the gravel until the tray is almost full. Then it drains back through the pump into the tank; passing through a plastic screen to prevent gravel from getting into the pump.

Sometimes the perforated pipe or hose is used just for return drainage and the solution is pumped out over a hose running along the top of the gravel.

Circulation of Nutrient Solution

My own system is the simplest of all and it works. I have no drainage groove or hose or tile in my trays at all. They are flat-bottom trays. I pump the nutrient solution through a hose running over the top of the gravel. It discharges at the far end of the tray, which is raised above the near end by just enough so that the solution will run back by gravity-flow toward the tank.

I have a drain hole in the near end of the tray. There is a valve there, but I keep it open all the time so the solution will run through just slowly enough to let the tray fill from the other end where the hose is discharging the solution. The length of time it takes for the solution to migrate back through all the gravel is just about the right exposure of nutrients to the plant roots.

I don't object to the perforated pipe or hose in the bottom of the tray for filling and for returning the solution, but it does present the problem of root infiltration so that you have to run a rotorooter through to clean it out from time to time.

Of considerable importance is the tank in which you hold your nutrient solution. In some countries this is

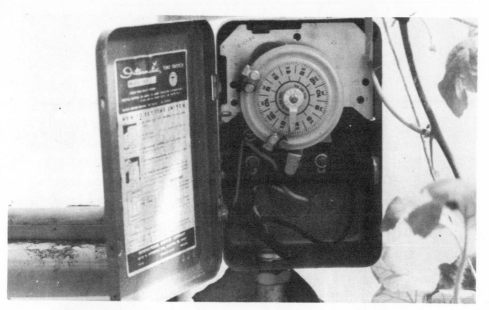

This simple timer is set to turn on the pump twice daily for automatic feeding of the plants.

At the bottom of this below-floor-level nutrient solution tank a submerged pump (lower right) has pumped the solution into growing trays (not visible) through long pipe and hose. The solution is now draining back into the tank by gravity flow.

created by digging a pit, then sliding down into it a big tank of plywood coated with fiberglass and resin. Some tanks are made of waterproof reinforced concrete. Some are simply plastic containers either above or below ground; just so the solution can be pumped from the tank into the trays and be pumped or drained back into the tank.

My tanks are made of plywood with a liner of poly-vinyl chloride or fiberglass and resin.

How large should the tank be? In a typical small commercial hydroponic "package" the growing trays may be about 3 by 12 feet in size and eight inches deep.

Author's commercial greenhouses typically have controls like those on the next three pages—for controlling the feeding, recycling, and discharging of the nutrient solution. Below, he is opening the valve of feeder pipe connected to hose that will carry nutrient solution over the top of the gravel and discharge it into tray at its far end. Solution drains back into collecting area (where liquid is seen) through screen-covered holes in gravel retaining board (left). This collecting area has a safety over-flow outlet seen in picture. However, drainage back into nutrient tank is through pipe connected to that lawn-sprinkler-type valve at the right. Note that pipe and fittings, wherever possible, are of plastic for less interaction with minerals in the nutrient solution.

The tank of nutrient solution to service such trays should be large enough to contain about 70 gallons of solution per tray.

In all your trays and tanks, remember not to use metal fittings for connecting your plastic pipes or hoses. Bronze or brass may be all right but fittings of copper, zinc, or iron will corrode in the nutrient solution and add a certain toxicity to the solution. Use plastic pipe, hose, and fittings. The PVC material used for plastic lawn sprinkler systems is fine.

Now I hope you will carefully study the photographs presented in this chapter with their descriptive captions.

Author's simple system for pumping nutrient solution to growing trays utilizes a hose running from nutrient tank over top of gravel. It discharges at far end of growing tray and runs by gravity flow back into tank.

These will help you to visualize the automated hydroponic gardening method better than any words.

Whether you buy or build it, the automated hydroponic greenhouse right in your backyard or other convenient location is your secret for the year-round production of fruits and vegetables of great beauty, with the highest nutritional quality, with minimum work and optimum enjoyment.

With pump running, author opens valve to eject used-up nutrient solution in order to clear tanks for fresh supply. Old solution is drained through hoses into outside yard for use on outdoor plants or lawns.

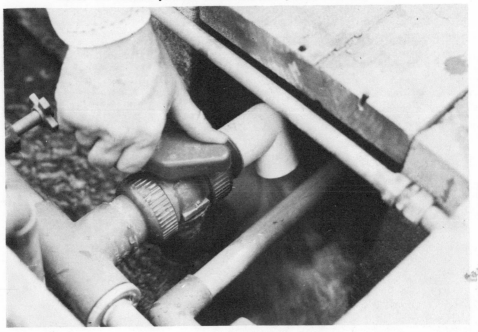

Planting By Design

Chapter 7

Planting By Design :

the most food in the least space

WHEN I TELL my classes or lecture audiences that a 10- by 12-foot backyard greenhouse will produce all the fresh produce needed by a family of four or five—year-round—some people are just a little bit skeptical.

But here are the secrets of that: first, in a greenhouse you can maintain optimum growing conditions winter and summer; and second, you can stagger or schedule the planting of various parts of your crops so that all year long you have just enough tomatoes, say; or lettuce, or green beans, for your family and not far more than you need.

119

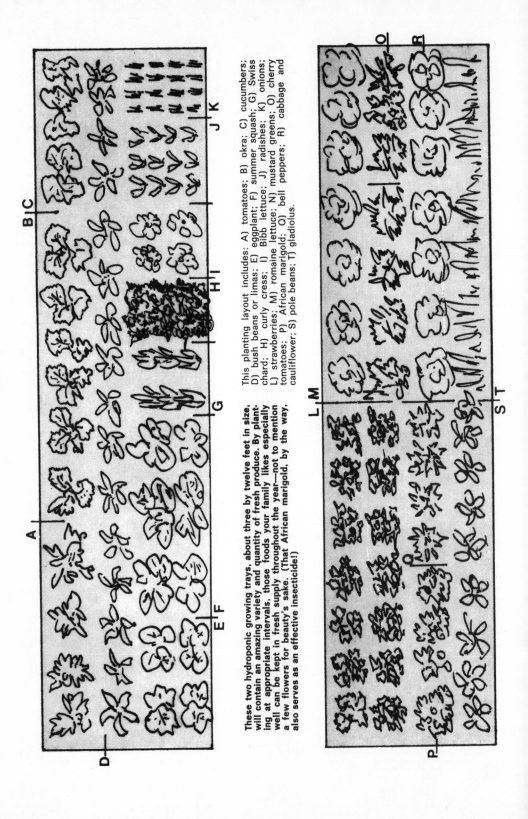

These two hydroponic growing trays, about three by twelve feet in size, will contain an amazing variety and quantity of fresh produce. By planting at appropriate intervals, those foods your family likes especially well can be kept in fresh supply throughout the year—not to mention a few flowers for beauty's sake. (That African marigold, by the way, also serves as an effective insecticide!)

This planting layout includes: A) tomatoes; B) okra; C) cucumbers; D) bush beans or limas; E) eggplant; F) summer squash; G) Swiss chard; H) curly cress; I) Bibb lettuce; J) radishes; K) onions; L) strawberries; M) romaine lettuce; N) mustard greens; O) cherry tomatoes; P) African marigold; Q) bell peppers; R) cabbage and cauliflower; S) pole beans; T) gladiolus.

Isn't that what often happens in ordinary gardening? Just when green beans are plentiful in the store, yours are coming on in the garden in larger amounts than you need. Then when yours are all gone, so are those in the store; or at least they have become so expensive again you forget about green beans until they are "in season" again.

Well, in that backyard hydroponic greenhouse of yours, you can arrange your plantings and control their environment, with very little effort, and have a living, growing, year-round fresh food producer you have to experience to really believe!

Let me give you a direct transcription from one of my classes to show you how your food production schedule can be worked out to suit your own family's desires.

Here we go, almost verbatim, just as if you were sitting in one of my classes:

● ● ● ●

What we're interested in right now is maximum utilization of planting space in the greenhouse. Let's assume our growing trays are about twelve feet long and three feet wide.

All right, Ole, what do you want to grow in your greenhouse?

"I want to grow tomatoes."

All right. You're going to grow tomatoes. Do you eat lots of them? Okay. How many plants do you want to start with? Three?

"No, I want two."

You want two tomatoes. Okay, let's put them down on your diagram here. This is a tomato here and this is a tomato there. Now in about a month you will plant two more, won't you? And keep them going that way all year. The growing space for that tomato is going to be about a square foot and for this tomato another square foot.

Now what kind of tomato are you going to plant? I'm not going to ask you to plant one that grows eight feet high and then you have to cut it off at the top. I'm going to ask you to plant one that comes up about a foot, then it branches naturally into two branches; then when it grows about another foot it branches naturally into two more branches. Okay? Sort of a candelabrum, isn't it? It will be a self-terminator at about six feet high. And it will have clusters of tomatoes everywhere. We call it Variety H-11.

Now, one of you gentlemen, what do you want to grow?

"Oh, let's have some celery."

You want some celery. Why do you want celery?

"You can make chop suey with it."

Okay, would you like to grow Napa celery?

"Yes."

All right. I'll tell you why I would approve that. Isn't celery usually about a 120-day crop? But some of the Napa varieties are about a 50-day crop, aren't they? Very tender, too. Now how much do you want of it.

"I'll have a half dozen stalks."

Half a dozen?

"All right, a dozen."

Hydroponically-grown tomatoes are almost universal favorites. Properly grown, they have superior nutritional quality, superb appearance, tender skin, firm flesh, delightful aroma and flavor, and remarkable keeping qualities. Dorothy Weeks fills her basket with some real beauties.

A dozen! How many salads do you think you can make with just one stalk of Napa?

"Two."

Two salads? Do you have 15 people in your family?

"Yes."

Okay, if you have 15 people in the family, then I'm sorry I spoke.

"He's got six kids that can eat a lot of food, that's all."

Okay. How many weeks apart? Not the kids; the celery!

"Oh, they ought to be a couple of weeks apart."

All right. Two weeks apart. But I'm going to let you plant only three now. Two weeks from now I want you to plant three more.

"Would that be from seed each time?"

Yes, sir. You could prestart Napa, but I would say from seed. What else do you want in your salad?

"Green peppers."

Green peppers. Well, now, you have me in a bind here. If you're going to grow green peppers you have to promise me you will work with the tomatoes one day and the peppers another. Because peppers can be host to some diseases that will knock a tomato out. So please remember that.

Do you want some curly cress for your salad? All right, let's put it out here on the front edge where we can get to it all the time. Put curly cress all over there on the diagram.

How about some Swiss chard?

"Good, very good."

You like that? Fine, some Swiss chard in here.

This young Swiss chard plant will grow large, yet tender—great either cooked as greens, or raw in salads!

"Spinach."

All right, do you want little leaf or big leaf?

"I guess the little leaf is tender."

About the 30-day type of thing. Okay, let's put the chard back here on the diagram and let's put the spinach between that and the curly cress. Now do you want some lettuce? Bibb lettuce?

"Sure."

Okay, fine. Now I've got some space in here to fill up. What would I put back there?

"Green beans."

I'm glad you mentioned it because that will go very well there, won't it? And how many green beans am I going to put in there? Well, let's just fill out that whole block. In front of that, how about some peas?

"Sure."

This block right in here, then, is for green beans, right? What variety? How about Kentucky Wonder greasy pod resistant. Or Top Crop.

"How about Blue Lake?"

Blue Lake is a terrific green bean. But why do I suggest Kentucky Wonder? It seems to bear well year around. It's not so selective as to the time of the year.

What else do you want in your salad?

"Parsley."

That would be a pretty border plant, wouldn't it? Fine, let's put it along here. Okay, now right here we put what? Some curly cress. Now, why not plant some asters right here. Want some asters? Beautify the place.

"Yes."

All right.

"Green onion."

Why green onion? They're a bargain at the store, aren't they?

"Yes, but you can't get them at the store with the same flavor as those you grow."

All right, how long are we going to leave them in? About 45 days? Then can we put them back at this margin, maybe? Is that all right? We'll put our onions back here.

Now, those bell peppers. You notice that the diagram shows two trays with an aisle between the two for

Kentucky Wonder beans can grow to a very large size in hydroponic gardening, if desired, and still retain a tender texture. Light-loving plants do best along the greenhouse wall where light is strongest.

A small, young bell pepper plant in this hydroponic growing tray already displays ten bright-green peppers!

working room. Let's put those bell peppers in this other tray—away from the tomatoes. Let's put in several plants. A bell pepper will bear for a long time. Who wants some eggplant?

Eggplant along here. Peppers over here. We add the onions in here now. Do you want some squash? Okay, what kind do you want?

"Crookneck."

Where are you going to get zucchini?

"Can't we have them both?"

I really don't want the crookneck in there with the zucchini. Why don't I? Do you like speckled squash?

A zucchini plant just keeps producing—crop after crop—in this hydroponic growing bed. Until one becomes accustomed to the "magic" of hydroponics, it is difficult to imagine these splendid, healthy plants growing in gravel!

"Speckled? Is that what it will do?"

Yes, but it's delicious. Okay, we're having a fight now over the zucchini. All right, let's just plant zucchini. Your family doesn't like zucchini? Well, mark that off right now. Change yours to butternut.

"All right."

You want some okra? There has to be okra here somewhere. You've got to have it. Good for you.

All right, let's have some more suggestions. You haven't given me anything to plant yet!

"How about some black-eyed peas and collard greens?"

These "tinker bell" squash, picked young and small are a gourmet's delight—sliced thinly, sauteed in a little butter or oil.

All right, we'll put those here. Now keep going. Give me some more things.

"I want some cucumbers."

You want some cucumbers! How many plants do you want?

"Three."

Okay, how about right back here on the wall of the house. But I'm going to give you only two cucumber vines. Why did I give you so many squash and not so many cucumbers?

"Because a lot of cucumbers grow on one vine."

Yes, but why did I give you so many squash?

"I don't know. We're going to have tons of squash!"

That's for encouragement.

"Do you mean that we're going to need to be encouraged?"

That's to encourage your neighbor and your mother-in-law and other people. Because you're going to have pans full of them to give away! And that's going to promote neighborliness! We need it, don't we?

"Yes."

Now what can you give away that's better than zucchini squash?

"Strawberries."

Strawberries. Where do we want the strawberries?

"You mean we're going to have strawberries?"

Sure, we'll have strawberries.

"How long do they have to grow?"

Well, do you like flowers?

"Yes."

Then we're just going to plant this whole border in strawberries.

"Can't you put them in a hanging basket?"

Sure you can put them in a hanging basket, George. You can put them in a strawberry barrel. There are many ways you can plant them, aren't there?

Now let me tell you something about a strawberry. How many of you ever ate a fresh one? There's a difference, isn't there? Somebody asked, doesn't it take a long time? You're not going to run out of work while you're waiting for strawberries, because how many minutes a day did I tell you that you would have to spend in this greenhouse?

"Twenty."

Even miniature citrus plants flourish in the hydroponic greenhouse environment, protected from the elements, nourished by nutrient solutions.

Then what will you be doing mostly in that green-house?

"Just admiring it."

Admiring it, yes. But besides admiring it, what are you going to be doing? You are going to be replacing the plants that have been used up, so to speak, in this rotating, year-round production system, aren't you?

When you pull up that Napa celery, what has to go in that hole?

"Seed for more Napa."

When you pull up that spinach for your salad, what has to go back?

Lettuce in its many varieties is a staple in the greenhouse salad crop—and the author advises using the entire plant for salad-making, including those tender inner leaves. Just pull up the entire plant, he suggests; then plant again in that space—keep it growing all year long.

"Spinach."

"Do you pull up the whole thing?"

Yes. Now here's one of my pet peeves. If there is anyone who drives me out of my mind, it's someone who grows some beautiful lettuce and then picks off and eats the oldest leaves first! I know some old-timers who have never eaten a fresh, tender leaf of lettuce because by the time they get all of the old ones eaten, they never get to the center!

A friend of mine tells me that he has an uncle who has never tasted anything but a rotten apple because he buys a box at a time and eats all those that are spoiling first. He wouldn't know what a fresh apple tastes like. Maybe he gets his cider that way!

I had a brother-in-law in the army one time in upstate New York. He went out and bought some fresh country eggs (you know how firmly they rise in a frying pan?); well, because this egg didn't flatten out and run all over the pan he thought something was wrong with it. He was used to eating the old storage eggs.

Now a really delicious thing is black-seeded Simpson or Bibb lettuce with the whole plant pulled up, chopped and put into a salad.

Why are you growing this stuff? To be chintzy? To save it? I also had a great-grandmother in Kansas who never ate anything but moldy butter. She always kept the butter in the cellar and kept trying to eat the moldy butter up first. She never knew what fresh butter tasted like.

"Is this plant all going into the salad at one time?"

"The roots and all?"

Yes, at one time! You don't want it in there all at one time?

"Sure, we'll have some more planted and growing."

You're going to rotate, aren't you? This way, one of these small greenhouses can produce all of the fresh vegetables — perhaps excluding some of the root crops — that an entire family can eat. It can do better than that if you are really efficient.

"How big are they?"

Rhubarb? Just try some of this hydroponic variety for a real taste treat! This young plant will produce juicy, tender stalks.

The greenhouse? The one we are planning is 10 by 12 feet. But your actual planting space is only 67 square feet! But, see how you really utilize the space. When you come to the edge of this tray, do you have to stay six inches from the edge? No, plant right up to the edge.

So there are your strawberries! Now I still have a lot of planting space left. Do you want me to put in some

If you hail from the South, or just like it anyway—this tender young okra plant should suggest some of the possibilities of hydroponic gardening.

leaf lettuce somewhere? All we have so far is Bibb lettuce. Okay, all of the lettuce you want is going to be right in here.

You can plant some root plants. The kind that tend to grow above ground, like turnips. But carrots are a bargain at the store, aren't they? The quality is pretty good.

"You can't buy beets at the store like these you can grow."

All right, do you want to put in some beets?

"Yes, sir."

Okay, how many beets do I want you to plant?

"A dozen or so."

How often? Will you want a dozen beets every week?

"I'm not going to eat them."

Well, you are, too! Do you know why you're going to eat them? Because they won't have a bit of dirt on them. There won't be any sand on them. And you can take them right out of there, top and all, when they're only this tall; the beet, the top—everything.

"Top and all?"

Sure, and have something delicious. They don't have to be pickled; they don't have to be sliced; because at that age—when do they have the most nutrition, ladies?

"When they're young."

Why do we sprout seed, for goodness sake? Simply because we'll get more nutrition from the seed, right? So I'll give you a block of beets here. Now, you've got some space left, what are you going to do with it?

"I like radishes."

All right, how many radishes do you want?

"Quite a few."

Do radishes take a lot of space? They're going to grow quickly, aren't they? And the turnover can be rapid. Okay, put the radishes up here. Let's see, what did we have in this little spot?

"Curly cress."

Okay, it can stand the door of the greenhouse flying open pretty well. And so can the radish. So I want you to put the radishes up here.

"How about some sweet corn?"

I had rather not.

"How about asparagus?"

It takes two years for your crown to form so you would have to go out and buy a two-year-old crown. How are you going to clean it up enough to put it in the greenhouse? It is host to lots of diseases. Your asparagus will do very well outdoors. So, in the yard, close to where you're going to dump the nutrient solution after you've exhausted it, put in a sand bed, put your asparagus crown in with bark mulch and water it with the nutrient.

"How about cauliflower in the greenhouse?"

That's fine. Cauliflower, cabbage, broccoli — good, I'm glad you mentioned it because we have a lot of space we can devote to that.

"Why not corn in there?"

Because if I were growing corn in a greenhouse, I would grow nothing but corn, although some gardeners do have corn among the other plants.

"You must have a reason."

I do. Anyone want to guess?

"Pollination."

Pollination.

A young broccoli plant with its nutrient-rich flowers begins to emerge from its gravel growing bed.

If you put in a 57-day corn, just two rows at a time every week or ten days, within five weeks you can start to have continuous corn (because you'll gain about 15 days in this controlled environment). And what's the difference in the quality of the corn?

"It's beyond comparison."

You can't imagine it, can you? You wanted to sit in the greenhouse and watch the plants grow! Why, I even want you to have a little stove there with a kettle of boiling water. I don't even want you to go to the house with that corn! I want you to take it off, put the shucks in a paper bag and close the top with a little twister, and

Although the author prefers not to plant just a few stalks of corn in a variegated greenhouse crop, it can be done if you wish. Here are a few stalks growing in a plastic bucket! At the right are round, lemon cucumbers in the background, more cucumbers and tomatoes.

then cook the corn right there. Hand it out the door right to your family! You're going to experience a tremendous taste difference that you can't imagine.

Are you going to eat it raw? Don't laugh; people do. Anyway, have your kettle ready in the kitchen, because the less time from stalk to plate the better. One time a lady came to my place and got some corn from me. She came back about a week later and I said, "How about some more corn?" "No," she said "I've still got some in the crisper." What a waste of time! I almost shot myself. Very disappointing — because what a difference when the corn is fresh!

Now this planting scheme we were working out. Did we include the plants everyone wanted! Okay.

But what are some of the factors that suggested the best way to arrange this planting chart? One is: how much light does a plant need? Does lettuce need much light?

"No."

Not as much as some other things. It's a lower light plant. Remember I put tomatoes to an outside wall. Where did I put the green beans?

Outside wall.

Okay, but I put the peas in front of the beans, didn't I? Lower light level. What did I tell you about the door opening? Near the door we put some curly cress in one tray and some radishes on the other. Why? Because they can stand the buffeting of that door opening and closing.

Now, about plant variety. What is the importance of plant variety?

"Some do better in one place than another."

Peas, needing less light than pole beans, can be planted alongside them
—in their shadow, so to speak—in the growing trays. Sugarpod peas do
well. The author encourages the planting of Chinese peas with their
edible pods.

Southern California, for example. Many of the plant varieties in southern California come from Greece and Lebanon — the parent plants. Not many potatoes there. Every part of the country has some special factors that affect one's choice of plant variety, just because of general climatic conditions.

But there are still other factors related to greenhouse gardening anywhere. The H-11 tomato, for example; a good size for a small greenhouse. It doesn't grow 15 feet high. It gets to about six feet and then stops; and that's an ideal height in this situation.

What about green beans? Now everyone voted for Kentucky Wonder, but what if you have a smaller greenhouse unit where you can't grow green bean plants with that much height?

"Bush beans."

Bush beans. And what's the difference between a bush bean and a Kentucky Wonder? The vine height, isn't it? How old can you let a bush bean get?

"I don't know. The gophers always ate mine."

You're not going to put a gopher in your greenhouse, are you? I haven't tried all the varieties of the bush bean. But I know that some bush beans can be five years old and still be putting out the same production. The vine can be pruned and cut back.

What about peas? How about some Chinese peas? And in what season do your little Chinese peas grow out of doors?

"Autumn."

All right, but they will grow pretty well amost into hot weather, won't they? So it's a pretty good year-round producer. So I would prefer it over the sugarpod

A tasty harvest of green beans fills this pail to overflowing — the product of sound plant nutrition.

pea in some instances, because you can eat it pod and all, can't you?

If you want some varieties anyway, regardless of their height, you just have to do more pruning. If you don't prune some of these climbing types of tomatoes, they'll go to 25 feet. They don't produce as much fruit either, when they have such runaway growth.

Remember that in some instances, the difference between a bush and a tree is that the top was cut out. It's the same in producing some tomatoes, green beans, and other plants.

Another point on plant variety. What kind of radish do you want?

"Icicle?"

Mainly you want a sweet one, don't you? So the fastest growing one is the best one. The white globe is a good variety. What varieties of lettuce are you going to use?

"Bibb lettuce."

Bibb lettuce is very good because it comes to a loose head. In a hydroponic garden you are going to grow a much more tender lettuce than you ever grew outdoors because the main enemy of the lettuce is high temperature and dehydration. I'd like to see you use Bibb and romaine as well as leaf lettuce in the salad bowl.

"Does the yellow string bean take a long time to grow?"

No. You can get a good wax bean in about 57 to 63 days. So that means you can plant those vines, say, two weeks apart and you would have four stages coming on. Do you eat a lot of them?

"Yes."

Well, that's one thing we want to do. This lady says that in her home they eat lots of wax beans. So that certainly is one of the things for her to grow. But don't grow those things that are of low frequency in coming across your table. How much parsley do you eat—or how much would you eat if you had fresh parsley right out of your greenhouse? That is one consideration. Some of the things you buy in the store are two weeks old when you get them, and thus are not such favorites with your family. But minutes-fresh from your own garden and the family may really go for them.

Another question about plant variety relates to the

One doesn't ordinarily think of watermelon as a greenhouse crop, but this miniature, hanging variety takes little horizontal space—and is a delicious treat.

Pineapple in New England? If the environment is maintained at supportable levels in the hydroponic greenhouse, almost anything is possible!

nutrients you will use. Some varieties respond better to nutrient solutions than others.

Why would I want a specific variety of cabbage?

"Weather and temperature."

Weather and temperature. What else? Production time. The time it takes for production. Another factor: It is important to buy seed developed for your part of the country. If you want to buy some Burpee and you're in the East, buy from Philadelphia. If you're in the West, buy from Riverside. If you're in the Midwest, it is Clinton, Iowa. That's just an example. Buy the variety that's going to thrive in your area and pay attention to the specifications in the seed catalog. They are usually accurate. What specifications will the catalog give you?

Time for production, for example. If it says 57 days you can believe it, except in the greenhouse that may be speeded up a little.

What else is the catalog going to tell you? It should tell you if the variety is resistant to certain diseases. Remember, I told you that if you wanted green beans in your hydroponic garden use a variety that is resistant to greasy pod mildew.

That mildew is going to be nonexistent until when? I'll tell you. Until about two days before you're going to harvest those beans! It's just that sneaky. Somehow it gets the news and knows when to be there.

Have any of you ever had that problem with relatives? They can sure tell when you've got plenty of groceries. Then there's one relative I love to have come to see me. He brings groceries. Can you imagine that?

"Does he have a greenhouse?"

No, he doesn't have a greenhouse. He's retired. He lets other people run greenhouses. He's the pessimist that finances some of us optimists!

"I was wondering; you mentioned that some vegetables aren't economically grown in a greenhouse. Why? And what are some of them?"

Well, you have to think of the quality and price of some things available in the stores and ask yourself if you want to use the time and the space in your greenhouse to grow them.

Potatoes, for example, are still a great bargain. A hydroponic potato wouldn't be any better than the russets that are shipped from Idaho. The potato is a wonderful, wonderful thing. It's a root crop that stores well.

Radishes are usually a bargain. Most of the root crops,

A variety of food plants showing a full-scale growing plan in operation. Not all of them are distinguishable in this photograph, but in just this corner of Dr. and Mrs. Stoops' garden are tomatoes, eggplant, bell pepper, and yellow summer squash.

This corner of the garden shows some plants in ordinary flower pots with a sand and sawdust mixture fed regularly with nutrient solution. Here are cucumbers, oakleaf lettuce, peas, kale, bell pepper, chard, and Chinese lettuce.

in fact, should be grown hydroponically only if you just really want to have them in your garden.

But all of the leafy vegetables, like cabbage, lettuce, chard, spinach; and all of the fruity vegetables like eggplant, pepper, tomato; and the beans and peas—certainly you would grow those.

It's not that you can't grow the others hydroponically. If you were in an area where they weren't available with good quality at a low price, you certainly would.

On some of the U. S. Navy's submarines there are hydroponic units in which they grow everything. There, incidentally, you would probably change from a gravel-culture method to a straight water-culture method.

"Is there a particular time to grow certain vegetables hydroponically? Or can you grow all year?"

All year-round for most of them, but try to use seeds of varieties that do best at certain times of the year—even in hydroponic gardening.

It is very interesting that the seeds we are using today have been so designed that we have varieties for every season. Twenty years ago there wouldn't have been so much incentive to do hydroponic gardening because at that time we didn't have the seeds that we have today and we didn't have some of the mechanical devices used in hydroponics available at a reasonable price.

●   ●   ●   ●

There you have a good example of the way my class sessions usually go—and a pretty good idea of how you can really make even a small hydroponic garden an almost perpetual cornucopia of healthful, gourmet foods specifically designed for your family's taste.

Starting Plants And Seeds

Chapter 8

Starting Plants And Seeds:

getting your hydroponic garden under way

MOST OF THE plants in your hydroponic garden can be started from seed. In some cases the seed can simply be dropped onto the top of the gravel in your growing trays. It will slip down into the crevices and receive ample moisture as you flood the growing trays twice a day.

In other cases you will want to start the seed in separate starting media, like peat moss—the Jiffy Seven pellets from Norway are a good example. You can get them at nurseries and seed houses.

They are little peat moss wafers about three-eighths of an inch thick and about two and a quarter inches in diameter. They expand when wet to a thickness of about two inches.

Starting Pellets Are Convenient

With these pellets you don't have to go through all the problems of making a flat of potting soil. You plant the seed right in the pellet. When the plant is well started you put the whole slug of peat moss with the plant growing on top of it right into the gravel. You couldn't have a neater system. When you are ready to

Jiffy Pellets offer a quick and easy way of prestarting those plants best not started by placing seed directly in the gravel. Here a young okra plant is almost ready for transplanting.

remove the old plant, just pull and the whole root system growing around this moss pellet comes out. It stays intact —doesn't mess up your hydroponics system with lots of roots remaining in the gravel.

These little pads also come in small trays. You can put water in the tray. The water will migrate all around

You can plant the seed right on top of the pad. Remember, put two or three seeds on each pad, keep putting water in the bottom of the tray, and the seed will germinate with moisture drawn up from the bottom.

That means you never have to get water on the little

The entire Jiffy Pellet, with its prestarted okra plant, is set into the gravel-filled growing tray and covered slightly—just as if the gravel were soil.

seedling. Why is that important? Water mold can't develop. The drier you keep the little plant itself, the better.

You can start plants that have to be prestarted this way right in the greenhouse if you want to, and I think that is ideal because you have a good environment.

Extra Attention to Seedlings

However, if you run a very busy household the seedlings may be germinated a lot more easily right on the drainboard in your kitchen. It is true that the greenhouse system is automatically looking after your growing plants, but your seedlings may need a little additional water or other attention and individual care, so there actually may be some advantage in starting them in your house.

You know, you can learn a lot and derive some enjoyment just from germinating seeds. You can experiment with the effects of presoaking, for example. Presoaking seeds will usually save some time. This is especially true on seeds of the melon, squash, and cucumber family; or the hard seeds, okra or seeds of that type—presoaking does save some time.

But also remember that the seed is quite marvelous in the way it takes up moisture naturally. And you have time, really. Seeds are harder to handle after they're wet, and it's easier to get bacteria on them. So even though you may enjoy this kind of experimentation, as I have, you probably will conclude, as I have, that natural procedures are really better. If you rush everything, you will find that the seeds begin rushing you

Small seeds may be started in hydroponic gardening simply by scattering the seed in the growing area. They drop into the crevices and are moistened by the nutrient solution as it circulates through the gravel.

and you will have to move fast after you get them going.

In starting seeds, it is important to keep air circulation good and not to get things overly wet. You also have to be careful not to cause physical injury to the tender young plants.

Some Plant-Starting Techniques

Let's look at some specific plants and how they are best started. Lettuce seeds, for example, can just be scattered around on top of the gravel and, later, thinned. Similar plants like curly cress, chard, spinach—the same way. Cucumbers should be started in a peat moss pad or in a sand cup then inserted in the gravel. Beans will start very well just pressed down into the gravel. Squash, too, will germinate that way.

If you buy plants already started, like tomatoes, you have to be certain you don't bring plant diseases into your greenhouse. Wash those plants to the bare root! Just wash them in plain water, then insert them carefully into your moist gravel.

Besides the problem of disease in using plants pre-started in soil, you have the problems inherent in changing to a different type of watering system, as well

Larger seeds can be pressed down into the gravel to just the level where they will receive moisture from the nutrient solution. Some "hard" seeds can be presoaked, but the author prefers to let nature take its course.

If plants prestarted in soil or other unsterilized media are planted in the greenhouse, the roots should be washed thoroughly of all the original material—to avoid bringing in disease organisms.

The author believes in beautification of one's working environment! Here he plants a gladiolus bulb (peeled of its outside husk) directly in the gravel tray. (Note hose for delivering nutrient solution running along center of growing tray over top of gravel.)

Young gladiolus plants shoot up from the gravel just as they would from the soil. Note the spacing between plants.

In all their glory, gladiolus or other flowers in the greenhouse are important, the author believes, for their aesthetic value. After all, working in the greenhouse garden should be food for the soul as well as for the body!

as the problems of dissimilar soils. Sometimes people will buy a citrus tree that was balled in clay and plant it in sandy soil. They will water it faithfully, but what happens? It dries up because the roots haven't left their ball of clay and gone into the sandy soil. Dissimilar growing media.

The other problem in using dissimilar growing media is the bacterial problem I mentioned. There are two types of bacteria: aerobic and and anaerobic. If you have a prestarted plant growing in a little mud ball and place that tightly packed little mud ball in gravel, you're going to get some anaerobic bacteria in your greenhouse. Some secondary plant pathology will develop and you will possibly get some bacterial root disease.

So wash off the soil or moss or whatever your prestarted plants came in and place the roots into your own clean gravel.

Use Enough Seed

In starting plants, don't be stingy with seed. If you want one plant in a given place and you put in one seed and it doesn't come up, you have a vacant spot when some good food could be growing.

You therefore have to become a "murderer"! I want you to plant three seeds in a spot, then pull out the two weak ones.

Some plants you will propagate from root tissue or other plant tissue rather than seed. For example, you can cut the bottom off a celery stalk and plant it, root and all. Have you ever planted the top of a pineapple? Terrific! I used to go to a supermarket and get all of

Some plants are started from plant tissue rather than from seed or bulbs. Bill Haas shows a pineapple top getting a good start in a flower pot, fed by nutrient solution.

their trimmings—sell them a few months later for $1.95 as ornamental plants.

Do you know what happened one time? I forgot some of them in the greenhouse. A few months later they were still there, being watered and fed while the other things were being fed. Little pineapple developed on those stems. I sold those plants with tiny pineapples on them to a man in the motel business. He was really proud of them. I was too. I was so proud of them, in fact, I asked $15 each! He paid it. He called me the next day to ask for two more. Two nuts in his bar that evening had spotted the plants and cut off the little pineapple with a pocket knife! Well, that's business.

Now if you use roots for propagation, what are you going to make sure of? No disease. You're going to be very careful where you select them, aren't you? What are you going to wash these things with? If you don't have any other disinfectant, soap and water will do nicely. But clean the things up before you take them into your greenhouse and propagate them.

How are you going to cut up the root pieces? With a clean knife; a sharp, clean knife. Dip the knife in soap and water between cuts, or run it through a flame.

Extra Help for Transplantation

There is another important factor here. After the seedling develops, you may want to "kick" it with a little extra nutrition. Some of your nutrient solution formula at half dilution will be about right. Do this just before you transplant the seedling, because you want to do something called hardening, or raising the osmotic pressure. How do you raise osmotic pressure? By leaving the same amount of salts in the plant but without the same volume of water. In other words, you are going to make it a little saltier. If I give you a lot of salty popcorn, what are you going to want next? Water.

So if I get this plant salty and I put it into the gravel growing medium, what is it going to want? Water. And it will start growing rapidly. Incidentally, smaller plants or seedlings take off better than larger ones. Don't let your seedlings get too large. There is also more chance of injury to the roots of your seedling when you thin out the weaker ones. Basically, however, the earlier a plant can begin developing its root system in the environment in which it will mature, the better.

I haven't, by any means, attempted in this chapter to give you a complete course in the starting of plants. What we have done is to discuss some aspects of plant-starting that are of special interest in hydroponic gardening.

Whether you scatter seeds of certain plants on top of the gravel, like lettuce; or push them into the gravel, like beans; or start them in Jiffy Pellets or some other starting medium for transplantation—or whether you start from a root or a crown—you are going to marvel at the power the Creator has placed in living things and be well on your way to the sheer delight of watching those plants develop in the ideal environment of the hydroponic greenhouse garden.

Making Your Garden Grow

Chapter 9

Making Your Garden Grow:

more on hydroponic techniques

THE BEAUTY OF modern hydroponic gardening is in its control of the factors affecting food production. Think of the factors the successful gardener has to control if he is going to have the kind of food that delights the soul and envigorates the body!

There is the fungus and mildew problem. What if the crop doesn't get watered? Nutrition can affect food production. Lighting, quality of seed, negligence, even careless neighbors can affect food production. Right?

But fortunately, plants are pretty tough. God made them tough. And, with your hydroponics system keep-

169

ing the environment under control, if you don't have a crop it's because you're not planting!

Planning for Maximum Results

Perhaps the most important of all factors affecting food production is planning.

We have talked about planning the greenhouse in relation to location, for example. If you have a choice, where will you locate a greenhouse? Next to a coastline or away from it? Away from it, right? Land may be cheaper, not too much fog, more light.

We have talked about planting in relation to humidity control. Some people ask me about putting a humidistat in the greenhouse. I don't put one in mine because my greenhouses are cooled with evaporative coolers which bring in some humidity with the air. About 50 percent humidity is desirable. Can I maintain 50 percent humidity? Not when it's raining, because I have to have some outside air and the humidity outside may be much higher. So a humidistat would be a waste of money, wouldn't it? Not good planning. Unless, of course, you're out on a desert. Then you might want to plan a humidifying system to bring in a little moisture in case you're not building up enough humidity internally.

If you live in a very rainy climate where you have high humidity all the year around, then you would have to have a good heater to help keep things dry.

What about being careful to get the best plant varieties—those varieties that will do best in a greenhouse environment in your locality? Here your seed supplier, your county agricultural agent or your university agricultural extension service will be of great help.

Some tomatoes, for example, will set better fruit at low humidity. Some will set better at high humidity. Some of them with less daylight. Some of them with cooler temperatures. If you know you're coming into a time of year with low daylight or a long period of cloudy weather, you simply change the seed variety.

As a part of your planning, visit someone who is already operating a greenhouse, a successful one. Tell him what you are planning to do. You know what kind of information he'll give you? Honest, direct information.

Caring for some plants, particularly if you are growing them in individual pots or other containers, will be made easier if you place them on convenient workbenches rather than on the greenhouse floor.

Because anyone who has been through the same thing you are planning is going to be interested in your plans and your success, isn't he?

Cold Weather Heating

How do you plan for heating in cold weather? I prefer natural gas to butane or propane. It has fewer detrimental effects on plants. Of course a reputable butane-propane dealer who sells the proper appliances for a greenhouse can equip you so that you can use these gasses safely.

If electrical heating is cheaper in your area, it is very good. Steam heating, hot water heating, as we mentioned earlier—with tubes buried in the greenhouse floor; use what is most economical.

What other environmental effects do we need to take into account in our planning? What about places where there is a high wind a great deal of the time? What about those of us who used to live in Oklahoma? We lived in eternal hope back there. We got our fields ready and put in the crop we thought we were supposed to put in. In those days anyone who used fertilizer was downright sinful. Not that anybody went to church; they just didn't want to be sinful. Well, they would put in the best corn they could select from the crop before, and cultivate three times before hot weather came. They would have it all beautifully cultivated, then around the fifth or sixth of July—you could count on it—the searing winds came up from the south. And they just burned up the fodder, didn't they? They dried up the silk. They shattered the tassels. And that was your corn crop.

My grandfather was a specialist. He grew "nubbins." Not because he wanted to—everybody in that country grew nubbins. We were the nubbin capital of the world. Then, why didn't he grow something besides corn? Simply because back in Kentucky he grew corn and out in Oklahoma he was going to grow corn. There were a lot of crops that would have done better, right?

Be wary of tradition because you may just stumble blindly into difficulty with the environment.

What about areas where there is a high incidence of disease? What if the corn crop had smut, and blight? Why then plant corn at all? Aren't there a lot of other things we can grow?

Environmental Control

But that's talking like an outdoor gardener, isn't it? All of the problems you can mention are just that many more reasons for using a greenhouse. Because in a greenhouse, can we rule out the wind? Yes. We can rule out the shattering effects of too much rain, can't we? We can rule out most of the diseases. We can certainly control the temperature, humidity, and ventilation.

Of course there are always those accidents that can't be avoided! I had a friend who was growing orchids in a greenhouse, a large crop. He had called the butane man to make sure that the butane was delivered in December one year. It didn't get delivered. What happened to his orchids? Mush, that's right! And a big clean-up job!

What other, perhaps personal factors have environmental effects? Your own comfort, that's one. What happens when I walk into a greenhouse and it feels too muggy for me? I open the vents and bring in some fresh air. But do I consider whether it is uncomfortable for me or is it uncomfortable for the plants? I should think first of the plants' comfort, shouldn't I? But I do know that I have skin, just as a plant has. Can a plant sunburn? Yes. Can its skin be injured? Can you break the plant's skin and infect it if you have some disease on your hands? Yes.

Then the plant, after all, is somewhat akin to us. The one thing that we must always remember is that plants are living things.

We don't hesitate to provide ourselves with the best environment we can manage for our own healthful development. Let's do the same for our plants.

Is the nutrition of your plants a vital part of their environment? You bet! Well-nourished plants flourish and provide high-nutrition food for you and your family.

Here is one of the greatest advantages of modern, automated hydroponics—you can know for sure that your plants are consistently receiving optimum nutrition, automatically, with minimum time on your part for checking the solutions and replacing them from time to time.

Review of Major Factors

Let's review some of the major factors here and add some important additional points.

First, let's review the pH characteristics of your water, for this affects plant growth and their ability to utilize some of the most important nutrients in your solution.

Your pH should be tested every four days. You will remember that this is a measure of your water's relative alkalinity-acidity. We try to keep the pH within a more or less neutral range just above 6.0, if we can. In areas where water tends to be alkaline, or hard, this means adding a little sulphuric acid now and then to offset the alkalinity of the water. Nitrogen is quite available to the plant with the pH up to 7.0, isn't it? Is phosphorous still available at 7.0? Yes it is, as well as potassium, sulphur, calcium, and magnesium. But at 7.0 the availability of iron to the plant is cut in half; same with manganese, boron, copper, zinc, and molybdenum.

Now, if the pH shifts slightly to the acid side, say over to 6.0, some other nutrients are not so available.

Nevertheless, there are acid-loving plants as well as alkaline-loving plants, aren't there? So for an all-purpose greenhouse with a varied crop we want a pH that strikes the best balance. Am I going to worry about it if it goes from 6.2 to 6.5? No, nor if it goes to 7.0. But I will worry about it at 7.5. Because I will have cut down on the availability of iron, manganese, boron, copper, zinc, and the other elements we mentioned. I want that pH to be, ideally, somewhere near 6.5 for an area where the water has lots of calcium. Calcium raises the pH, right? Makes it more alkaline.

Now of all these elements adversely affected by a pH either too acid or too alkaline—nitrogen, phosphorus, potassium, sulphur, calcium, magnesium, iron, manganese, boron, copper, zinc, molybdenum—which are essential to good plant growth? The answer is: all of them.

As mentioned earlier, you can have your supplier make up your nutrient formulas to suit your water and

The author demonstrates another form of bromthymol blue pH test. First (above) he places a few drops in a sample of his water or nutrient solution; and (below) compares color of the solution with those in the glass tubes of the measuring device. The pH should be checked every four days and maintained within a range of 6.0 to 7.0 for a variety of plants growing simultaneously (see text).

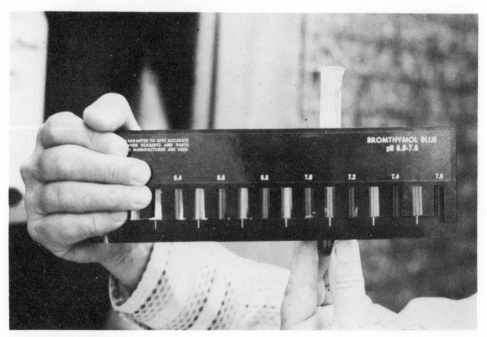

your crop; or you can, with experience, make your own.

The procedure is to test the pH of the water first, get it into an acceptable range—by adding small amounts of sulphuric acid if it is too alkaline—then put in the nutrients. Then test the pH again. Adjust it again.

Remember that you can test the pH with a paper tape called Nitrazene, available at garden shops, or with more elaborate devices illustrated elsewhere in this book. The use of more than one system—one as a check on the other—is not a bad idea. There really is no need to purchase one of the more expensive electronic meters unless money is no object.

As a matter of fact, even a swimming pool testing kit is all right if it will read low enough, at least as low as 6.0.

There is much more that could be said about the pH of your water and your nutrient solution—I hope this book will inspire you to study, to read, to talk with other successful growers. Learning is a never-ending process.

More on Nutrient Solution

Now—the nutrient solution itself, and how you use it. We've mentioned the various kinds of tanks it can be kept in. We've talked about manual irrigation of the growing trays by elevating the tank, then lowering it to let the solution drain back into the tank.

We have also talked about the more ideal, automated system with your nutrient tanks below the floor level of your greenhouse, the nutrient solution pumped automatically—at preset times—into the growing trays, then returning to the tanks by gravity flow.

You feed the plants just twice a day; that's enough. Your system is set to pump solution into the trays to just below the surface of the gravel.

Now, of course each time the solution is pumped into the growing trays, even though it drains back into the tanks, you have a little less solution. Thus, if you don't add water from time to time, you have, in effect, increased the concentration of the nutrients, haven't you? Because where does the water go in plant growth? It diminishes through plant transpiration and general evaporation.

You keep adding water; and, of course, that does dilute the solution, but usually not enough to make any difference for about six days. Then you discard your solution by pumping it outside the greenhouse and refill your tanks with fresh solution. Of course solutions can be mixed for different lengths of time. You could mix a 20-day solution or a 30-day solution. But it is very important that you keep adding back the water, keeping at least 90 percent of the original level so the nutrients don't become too concentrated.

Let's say, for example, that a plant is not taking all the calcium at a particular stage of its growth. If your water level goes down by half, then your concentration of calcium is twice as high. Why is that important? There are growth stages when the plants are rooting-in and they take different nutrients from the solution than they do when they are leafing or bearing fruit.

In hydroponics, we make sure that we present a consistent, balanced solution at all times, so the plant will have available what it needs when it needs it, but not in too concentrated a form.

So it is important to keep the water level up, prefer-

To avoid over-concentration of nutrients, it is important to add water as necessary to maintain your nutrient solution to at least 90 percent of its original volume during its useful life. A simple float-activated valve in the water supply line will do this automatically.

ably with a float valve of some kind, until it is time to discard the solution and replace it.

Pumping In and Draining Back

How long should you set your pump timer to run the solution into the growing trays? Time doesn't matter. The important thing is just to get it into the trays, up to just below the surface of the ground.

If it takes 45 minutes, fine. If your pump can fill the tray in five minutes, that's fine too.

How often? Usually something watered twice a day is better off than something watered five times a day.

Good drainage of the growing trays is important for adequate aeration of plant roots between feedings. If drainage is accomplished through a perforated hose or plastic pipe down the center of the growing tray, it should be cleaned of any root growth or dirt accumulation periodically with a rotorooter. If tray has a gentle slope toward the nutrient tank, gravity will accomplish the drainage with only a small outlet at the end, thus avoiding the problem of clogging.

In my own greenhouses, some trays are filled in 30 minutes, some in 15. It takes five hours for the trays to empty, for the solution to drain back, because my trays are very long. I pump all my nutrient solution up to one end of the tray and wait for it to come back by gravity flow. I use a hose over the top of the gravel up to the far end where it discharges.

Aeration Is Important

Now the drain-back is important. You can't leave the plant roots in the solution too long. They have to aerate, get oxygen.

What is the importance of oxygen? Well, there are some nutrients that your plants just aren't going to take if there is no oxygen present. I don't care how much boron you have in your soil, for example; if there is no oxygen present it can't be active and available to the plant.

The long, commercial trays may take five hours to drain back all the nutrient solution, but the solution is traveling down the length of the tray so all the plants aren't in water all that time. Smaller home trays drain back in 45 minutes. But, still, they don't need to be watered again for perhaps five or six hours.

Here's the thing about drainage and aeration. When I tell you that it takes a long tray five hours to drain back, remember that it takes 45 minutes for the water that's put in one end to get to the other end. That means that one end of the tray is getting watered almost an hour later than the other. So water is in motion all the time. Remember this, too; if you have a flat-bottom tray

and there is still a little solution in it after you are
through draining back, it isn't going to hurt; because
it is going to be replaced with fresh water how often?
Twice more the next day.

You can figure, in general, that it takes three times
as long to drain the nutrient solution back out of the
tray as it did to pump it in. If it were to take 30 minutes
to load, it would take an hour and a half to drain back.

Don't Feed At Night

One minor point, but still important. I don't want
to pump the solutions to my plants at night. Why? You
know about photosynthesis. Photosynthesis is the process by which the plant utilizes sunlight to convert all
the raw nutrient material into chlorophyl and that produces carbohydrates and sugars that go to the root.

So all day long, in the process of photosynthesis,
plants are taking in carbon dioxide and giving off oxygen. What happens at night? It reverses. And from
where does the carbon dioxide exude? From the roots
as well as from the leaves, because at night they take
in oxygen. However, the root is mainly giving off root
secretions and carbon dioxide. If the root is too wet at
night, you interfere with plant metabolism.

If you should run out of the nutrient solution you
have been using, don't substitute something else. You
are better off to let your system run on plain water for
a couple of days then to start your plants adjusting to
some other blend of nutrients.

Remember, although I said you could grow food
hydroponically without recirculating the nutrient solu-

tion, if you wish; I personally wouldn't consider a hydroponics system without this recoverability.

Besides the economy and convenience of it, if we don't recycle these nutrients the government is going to force us to do it. Right now we're talking about limiting the number of cows on a given amount of land because we are afraid of the nitrates that run off the land from manure.

Yet, at some point, you have to get rid of old nutrient solution. You circulate it through your greenhouse for six or ten days and then you have to pump it out and put in fresh solution. You can't bag it and haul it to the ocean!

So what do I do? Have you ever grown peas or apples or something like that? There's a time of year when you don't want the nitrogen to get to the apple, for example —in the winter—so it won't start premature growth on warm days. So how do you suspend the nutrients? You plant grass around the trees. The nutrient comes up in the green part of the grass stem and is suspended there.

In my particular situation, I grow grass by pumping my used nutrient solution out into a neighbor's pasture for the benefit of his prize black Angus.

Don't throw exhausted nutrients away. They are a lot better than whatever your trees or lawns are probably getting right now.

Temperature and Humidity

We should talk a bit more about temperature and humidity. In some greenhouses, humidity is supplemented by small sprinklers automatically controlled.

But for growing vegetables I don't believe I would use such a system. In fact, in a hydroponic greenhouse I normally don't worry about having adequate humidity, even in a dry climate. The evaporative cooler I use is bringing in some humidity.

True there are times when the outside air is unusually dry and it does become dry in the greenhouse, too— you remember I have a free-swinging louver for air pressure equalization. But a little dryness at times is a pretty good fungus, mildew, and mold preventative, isn't it? Besides, natural pollination occurs best when it is a bit dry in the greenhouse.

There is the reverse situation, too. When it's raining outdoors, I'd be silly to say that I could control the humidity at 50 percent—which is an ideal level for a broad spectrum of growing things.

Actually, in a well-stocked, vegetable-producing greenhouse, there is enough transpiration right around the plants to produce an invisible envelope of humidity, because the wind isn't whipping it around as it would outdoors.

In addition, the moistened gravel in the growing tray gives off a lot of humidity.

Regarding plant transpiration and that "envelope" of moisture, have you ever been in cornfield on a summer day when the corn is tall? Is it hot and humid in there? You bet it is.

Temperature control is one of the most important factors affecting food production. It is one of the best reasons for using an automated greenhouse that will go right on producing in- and out-of-season crops for you winter or summer.

In the summer heat, automatically controlled coolers —evaporative or otherwise—keep your plants from going into heat wilt or dehydration; keeps them growing in the optimum range.

In the wintertime, automatically controlled heaters help to maintain that ideal range; keep the plants from becoming dormant or actually freezing.

Again, let me say that for a variegated crop in year-round production, a temperature somewhere near 65° is ideal. But don't forget that you could have a greenhouse with low-temperature or high-temperature crops and that would change the heating requirements.

Hazel Bridwell checks some seedlings in her small year-round "spice-garden" greenhouse, heated by a wall-type gas heater. In mild climates, a small, thermostatically-controlled electric heater placed on the floor of the greenhouse may be entirely adequate to keep plants growing.

In a greenhouse operated in Oregon, the growers had stand-by propane heaters for use when the temperature fell to 27°. They were growing lettuce, broccoli, cauliflower—the cold weather plants. With those you can let it drop quite low. The reason I specify 65° is because for continuous production you will have a mixture of plants.

You know about caloric heat, don't you? You know about it in human physiology, at least. The same thing is produced in plants. You can freeze a bucket of water in an empty greenhouse when the outside temperature goes down to 29° or 30°. But you surely can't freeze it if the house is full of plants—because they are giving off heat. Also, because the plants are giving off heat, there is almost always a tiny motion of air in a greenhouse; warm air rising, and cool air falling.

Don't Always "Follow the Leader"

Now I told you to talk to other greenhouse growers and share information; but use your own good judgment and knowledge, too.

A fellow in Florida called me one night. He said, "My leaves are yellow. What should I do?

What is the first question you would have asked him? I asked, "On what part of the plant?"

He said, "Well, about two feet from the ground."

I said, "What does the tip look like? Has it quit growing?"

He said, "Yes."

I said, "Has it quit producing flowers?"

He said, "Yes."

"Not setting fruit?"

"Not setting any fruit."

"What's the temperature there?"

He said, "Oh, I guess it's about 38° out there tonight."

I said, "What about the heat in your greenhouse?"

"Heat?" he asked. "I don't have any heat; my sides are rolled up. And there is a breeze coming through here. It's about 38°."

I said, "Well, I would recommend that you roll the sides down and get the temperature inside the greenhouse up to 55°."

Do you know why he hadn't rolled the sides down and added heat? Because no one else in that area had! We do go from grower to grower to see what the other fellow is doing, don't we?

If we are going to grow out-of-season plants, we have to remember that it is out of season. If we are growing tomatoes in January, we have to remember how warm the nights are in the summertime when the tomato plant does the best.

What luck am I going to have raising cabbage in the warmest weather? Not much. Cabbage is a cold weather crop. So what can I do if I live in a hot climate and I want cabbage in the summertime? I can cool off the greenhouse, or I can possibly go to a different plant variety.

In growing varied crops simultaneously in a hydroponic greenhouse, we sort of split the temperature difference. Not too cold for the corn, beans, and tomatoes; not too warm for the cabbage and peas.

While we are discussing temperature and humidity we might as well say a little about light. You will recall that when we talked about utilization of space—optimum use of space—the location of some of our plants in the growing trays was governed by their relative need for light.

Light is one of the major environmental influences and a significant factor in our planning.

How much light does curly cress need? Well, if you can grow it in your kitchen, it must not need very much; so, you'll recall, we planted that seed along the inside edges of the trays. Remember, we utilize the planting space in some relation to light requirement.

Some people ask, "Do you use any artificial lighting?"

The analysis I have made of artificial lighting leads me to believe that in terms of increased production I would barely break even on the cost of the appliances and the electricity to run them. If artificial lighting would increase my production 15 or 20 percent I would surely use it. With some crops it will. But remember, we are basically concerned with varied crops grown simultaneously and most would not benefit that much from artificial light.

Avoid Physical Injury

Another environmental influence on plant growth is simply the physical handling of the plants.

You can be harvesting one crop and injure the crop next to it. If you ever want to be angry with yourself, just inadvertently set a flat of seedlings down on top of

Another example of effective use of vertical space—crucial to maximum greenhouse productivity. The author checks the appearance of a friend's lush pole bean vines as they begin their upward climb on twine attached to an overhead wire.

When a plant is exhausted, or when an entire plant (such as lettuce or spinach) is pulled up for use, roots come out clean from the gravel—one of the reasons gravel is the preferred growing medium. Plants should be removed when gravel is relatively dry, taking care not to injure neighboring plants. Note the relatively small root structure needed to nourish this large tomato vine. In hydroponics the nutrients are brought to the roots—they don't need to travel!

some other seedlings! Now, no one could be that stupid, could he? Except have I done it once? Probably a dozen times, and I will probably do it again sometime when I'm in a hurry. Yes, sometimes you, yourself, cause physical injury to your plants.

Remember that I told you not to be stingy when you get some leaf lettuce. Instead of just picking the outside leaves off I told you to pull it up by the root. Now what about the roots of plants next to it? How are you going to protect them? You're simply going to put your hand on the gravel around those plants that you don't want to disturb too much and pull out the roots of the ones you're taking. It may still disturb adjacent plants a little; but it isn't a big deal, because you're not pulling out a grapevine or something, you're just pulling out some very tender feeder roots.

Now, when a larger plant has run its course and you want to remove it to make room for the next crop, wait for that root to dehydrate if you can. Otherwise a great deal of gravel will come up with it and scatter all over the greenhouse. But if you'll wait until the gravel is as dry as possible it will come out much easier. Then you don't have much root tissue left in the gravel.

Now let's move on to one of the most fundamental aspects of successful hydroponic gardening; keeping your controlled greenhouse ecology free of injurious plant diseases and pests.

Good Housekeeping

Chapter 10

Good Housekeeping:

for the prevention of plant diseases and pests

I AM ALWAYS disturbed when I think of all the money spent on insecticides, fungicides, and bactericides that aren't needed and that won't do any good anyway.

Do you know that once garden plants become diseased there is nothing you can do for them? For some infections of the human body, we can take antibiotics that will destroy the infection. But with plants; well, I quit calling my pathologist friend to come out to tell me that I have an infection of some kind in those plants. Why? There is nothing I can do about it. But I certainly don't need it, do I? So what can I do?

I can practice good sanitation in the greenhouse and

195

take measures that will help my plants avoid diseases. I just don't need them to start with. The same goes for insects. So what do I do? I use preventive measures.

Who wants to spend a lot of money for just part of a crop? Yet people do it year after year because they don't do some of the basic housekeeping of good gardening. With good, clean gardening techniques you will have results like you imagine when you see those fabulous pictures in the seed catalogs.

When you plant some cabbage seed, are you going to have worm-eaten cabbages? Are they going to have to be doused with insecticides? Are they going to be loose heads? No. They're going to be tight, solid heads, free of disease, good to look at and good for you. What is going to happen if you plant a green bean? You are going to have beautiful, delicious green beans. Do you have a right to expect this? Of course. Should you expect anything less? No.

One of the main things I want to teach you in this book is housekeeping. If you have any propensity for housekeeping, you will be able to have good greenhouse crops. God fashioned an orderly world for us. If we do things in an orderly fashion we are in harmony with His creation.

Pre-planting Sterilization

One basic procedure in preparing a greenhouse and the growing media—the gravel tray—involves fumigation and sterilization.

Now I know that some people don't believe in this. Some people don't believe in vaccinations for human beings. If that is their bent, fine, but I can't help but feel that some of those people are either more skilled than I am or they are the luckiest people alive.

In all seriousness, I know people who have been gardening for 30 years and don't know what plant disease is because they've never had it. There are some people that human diseases just don't catch up with. If you are that lucky and don't want to sterilize—fine. But I recommend that we do.

In hydroponic gardening we are already avoiding so many of the problems we would have outdoors: dogs running through the plants, children riding bikes through, the plants don't get watered, or the wind burns them, or grasshoppers eat them . . . so many problems outdoors. But even though we have so many things in our favor indoors, let's get as many more things in our favor as we possibly can.

In ridding gravel, as a growing medium, from disease organisms and insect infestations, I use either methyl bromide, chlorine, sulphuric acid, or formaldehyde. Remember, I don't use these on plants. I use them to rid of all disease and pests the environment in which I will later grow my plants—hopefully without insecticides.

What happens when we fumigate or sterilize the gravel, the growing medium? We get rid of everything, don't we? Everything that could harm the plants. The result is that our nutrient solution is more effective; it promotes healthy growth without disease.

I am so careful about contamination of my greenhouse or anything in it that I am even extremely cautious about whom I allow to come inside. Even then I

"Helpful" neighbors may be one of the natural hazards of hydroponic gardening! What you have inside that greenhouse is so tempting—just to look at, mind you! Bill Haas knows, however, that even well-meaning neighbors and small children can inadvertently bring in plant diseases and pests. A good lock on the door is good crop insurance!

want them to be washed up real clean. Some greenhouse growers even use a different pair of shoes in the greenhouse.

At the greenhouses I operate, if I allow anyone to come in I ask him to step on some captan that I keep sprinkled on a little wooden platform in order to disinfect the soles of his shoes.

One should be very careful not to walk through grass before going inside the greenhouse. Grass may have rust or other contaminants. Also, one shouldn't move from working with petunias, nasturtiums, or mallow right into the greenhouse. These and other plants are host to lots of plant diseases.

Well-meaning neighbors can often be a menace in

this respect. They are always wanting to do something nice for you. They will often bring you plants just because they know you like them. If your neighbor brings you a nice plant, try to persuade him to take it back! In any case, put it outside the greenhouse door. Why? Because you are probably not a plant pathologist and let's just not chances that something in or on that plant will destroy the investment we have inside that greenhouse.

After all my warnings and cautions about diseases, you may by now be afraid to shake hands with your spouse! Well, it is almost that way with greenhouse

Many plant-disease agents are carried on the soles of shoes. Anyone entering a greenhouse should rub his shoes in a powder disinfectant like captan sprinkled at the greenhouse door. Some growers even change to special coveralls inside the greenhouse. Success in any hobby—or profession or trade—does require attention to the important details.

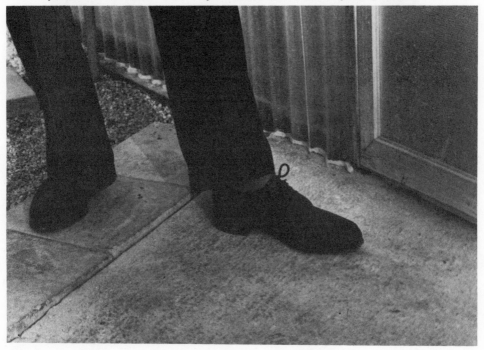

growing. After you have done a good job of sanitation you may be reluctant to invite anyone at all into your greenhouse. Gradually, however, you will overcome this fear and be able to enjoy the pleasure of inviting friends to see your outstanding plants. You will just be sure to use measures like those we have mentioned to prevent those friends from bringing in some contaminant.

Good Housekeeping Avoids Reinfestation

All right, what about reinfestation? If you have cleaned your entire greenhouse well and thoroughly fumigated the growing trays and gravel, continuing good housekeeping should prevent reinfestation.

Fungus, for example, requires an overly humid condition or some other condition favoring it, as in the incubation of any type of bacteria or mold. If you don't let such a condition exist too long—if you have good lighting; if you have good aeration of your growing medium; and if you use a fungicide, if necessary, for control—you won't have a fungus problem. If you walk past the exhaust fan of a greenhouse and smell something that smells exactly like dirty socks, you know mildew is present. You immediately use something to control fungus and mildew, like captan. You apply it right then and there without waiting to identify any particular type of fungus. Without immediate action, that fungus could spread through your greenhouse in 24 hours. It can work that fast.

Now, if I give a plant proper light, proper heat, proper everything, all the nutrition in the world and I go in some day and it just doesn't look as if it is getting proper nutrition, what has happened? Some alien organism has taken over. We've been invaded. What could possibly take over? Fungus and mildew, but what else? What about virus?

I told you earlier about the virus problem. It seems that whenever I call in a plant pathologist from the state or county agricultural department, it's always a virus. One time the virus turned out to be manganese deficiency. Another time I was treating a manganese deficiency and it turned out to be a virus. How are you going to know?

We can have a leaf sample tested by the government agricultural laboratories. We want to be specific, don't we? We can provide adequate nutrition and everything else, but if we ignore the possibility of disease invasion, we may be out of business.

First: Prevention

That's why my basic point regarding fumigation and sterilization is so important. I don't deal first with disease; I deal first with prevention. It's the same in the chicken business, isn't it? How many innoculations does a baby chick get? About six. You can't give that kind of "vaccination" to plants, but you can do your best to prevent any disease from getting a foothold.

Since we are talking about fungus and mildew, let's mention a few other relevant points. If you want to drive me crazy while I am working in my greenhouse, pick up some of my seed and let it run through your fingers. That will drive me right up the wall, because

I don't know whether you washed your hands or not!

Now, for your own sake, after you are through handling seeds, please don't put your fingers in your mouth. Seed producers are allowed to use material for seed treatment that we are not allowed to use in other types of pest control, right? Some of those materials are mercury compounds and, anyway, some of them taste pretty bad.

Sterilizing With Methyl Bromide

Let's talk about how to go about sterilizing your greenhouse environment. First, let's use methyl bromide. Remember that it is fairly dangerous material. Be sure to note all instructions that come with it. In simplest terms, you tightly cover what you want to fumigate— say your growing trays—with a plastic tarp, two to six mil thickness, and spray the methyl bromide underneath the plastic, about one or two pounds per 100 cubic feet. Do it very carefully, according to directions that will come on the container. As to the form of the material, I prefer Dowfum MC2—it's a mixture of methyl bromide and chloropicrin, which is a kind of tear gas.

When you put the plastic tarp over a growing tray, or whatever you are fumigating, make it air tight by taping down the edges with masking tape. By its odor, the gas

Fumigation of growing trays, easily and safely. The sequence of photographs on the next three pages illustrates the author's simple method of ridding the trays and the gravel growing medium of all harmful organisms before planting a crop: 1) the top third is cut off an ordinary plastic milk carton; 2) a piece of two-by-four cut to fit inside the carton has a nail driven into it, and the head cut off, and the shaft sharpened with a file; 3) the "spiked" piece of wood is in place in the bottom of the milk carton; 4) a pressurized methyl bromide soil-fumigation "bomb"

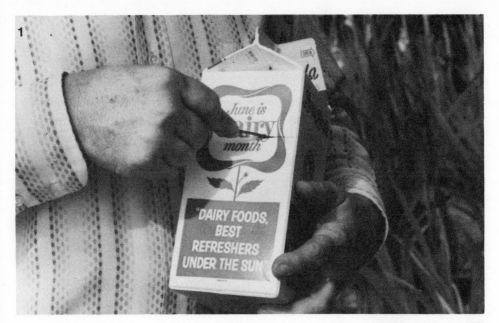

(read the label) is lowered into the carton—but don't press it down on that sharpened nail, yet!; 5) the growing trays are covered loosely with polyethelene plastic, its edges securely sealed with masking tape—with the "bomb" apparatus in place on the gravel under the plastic; 6) the "bomb" is pressed down hard on the sharpened nail which punctures the

bottom of the can, the gas begins to escape and infiltrate the gravel, securely contained by the plastic. Should any leaks be evident, have your masking tape handy to seal them, avoiding inhaling any stray vapor. The plastic milk carton contains any of the material that emerges in liquid form until it evaporates—preventing the over-sterilization of that

spot. This simple method enables the gardener to use this fumigation material without ever coming into contact with it. Just puncture the can, check quickly for any obvious leaks in the plastic, then walk out, lock the greenhouse door, come back in 24 hours, remove the plastic and aerate the trays for at least 48 hours (see text).

will announce to you very quickly if you have a leak in your tarp. Stop it quickly with a piece of masking tape. Leave covered for 24 to 48 hours. In another 48 hours, you can plant.

Again, let me caution you to be careful in using any kind of fumigant. Care for yourself and other creatures. I know one gardener who fumigated his cat. He didn't intend to.

I also knew of a carpet layer who had just finished a job and noticed a small bump under the carpet. He looked in his pocket and noted that his cigarettes were gone. Naturally, he thought his cigarettes were under that carpet. He certainly didn't want to take up all that carpet again, so he got a short piece of two-by-four and beat this bump down flat. The lady didn't even notice it.

But when he got outdoors he saw his package of cigarettes right there on the seat of his pickup. About that time, the lady came to the door and asked him if he had seen her parakeet! It seems that it had gotten out while she was cleaning the cage.

I'm not too sure how this applies to fumigation, except to emphasize the fact that you should know what you are doing. These materials are a bit dangerous. But don't let that frighten you out of using them for productive, disease-free gardening.

Remember that many of the things we use every day are dangerous. Couldn't you kill yourself with some of the things in your kitchen? And I don't necessarily mean the food prepared there! Do you have ammonia up on the shelf in a glass container? Get it down off the shelf. That container belongs under the sink so that when you pick it up it can't drop so far and break. You can imagine the possibilities of spilling ammonia in the Drano. We become accustomed to being careful with some things.

Sterilizing With Chlorine

For sterilizing the gravel in your growing trays, in addition to the things we have already discussed, you can also use chlorine—the same kind you use in a swimming pool. Use 13 ounces to 100 gallons.

How do you use it? You flood the trays, and plug the return drain holes for 24 hours. Be sure the solution covers the gravel in the tray. Remember—this is before you plant any crops at all—not while anything is planted in the trays. Then you have to dump the chlorine solution. Pump it out and down the sewer. Then flush the trays with clear water several times during a 48-hour period. Even then the gravel will smell a bit like chlorine, but that is nothing to worry about.

If, for some reason, your trays are constructed so that a substantial amount of liquid remains in the bottom— it will not drain out—you would be better off to use a gas like methyl bromide than a chlorine solution.

If you use the chlorine solution, how much will you need? Just compute the cubic-foot area of your growing trays and remember that there are seven and one-half gallons of liquid in a cubic foot.

If you don't have a tank large enough to prepare the chlorine solution in advance you can simply pour the chlorine, the right amount, as you have just calculated, over the gravel, then fill the tray with water. The chlorine will mix and produce a balanced solution.

Some people recommend the use of chlorine gas but I am personally afraid of it. If it is something you are accustomed to handling, all right; but that won't include many of us.

Methyl Bromide Preferred

Now, having discussed various fumigating and sterilizing agents, let me say again that after some years of experience I still prefer methyl bromide.

Methyl bromide is a gas. It comes in one-pound, pressurized cans, and you simply release it underneath the plastic you have taped to the top of your trays. Quick and easy. Just take normal care to avoid leaks and stop them quickly with pieces of masking tape if they do occur.

In using methyl bromide you may wish to use one of the special applicators sold for this purpose. Some clamp right onto the pressurized can, and puncture it as you twist it down. Then the applicator, a tube-like affair, can be inserted into the plastic material that covers your growing trays, or whatever you are fumigating. It is very safe to use. Some supply houses may simply loan or give you one of these applicators with the purchase of certain quantities.

A point worth remembering when you are using methyl bromide—use it when it is still cool in the morning. It will be easier to handle. At low temperature, it will come out of the can as a liquid and become a gas. Caution: if you spill some of this liquid itself on some gravel, forget about ever growing anything on that one spot. If you spill it on a glove, or a boot, or your leather overalls, or whatever—get that item of apparel off before the liquid soaks through and touches your skin.

As a fumigant, methyl bromide should be allowed 24 to 48 hours to penetrate the area being fumigated. Then the plastic cover should be removed and the area given full ventilation. That means all of your exhaust fans on for 48 hours before you plant something else.

One of the pressurized cans I told you about will take care of 100 cubic feet—or 100 square feet, 12 inches deep. This is more than enough for the growing trays in a small greenhouse.

So you are actually over-treating with the standard size can. But it doesn't hurt to over-treat as long as you catch any surplus in the liquid form in a pan or something so that it won't get into your growing medium; and that you allow a little extra time for aeration after the treatment.

Running water through the gravel growing medium from time to time after the plastic is removed helps in the aeration process.

Cleaning the Entire Greenhouse

Now, about the whole interior of your greenhouse. You should wash it down at first with a soapy water spray. Soap is a pretty good insecticide. But you don't want to build up a whole bunch of soapy film on the inside surface of your greenhouse, so follow the soapy spray with a rinsing spray. When I say soap, I mean soap. White King soap chips will be better for fighting bugs than a detergent will. Fels-naptha is also very good for cleaning up a greenhouse. You can also spray this soap solution on the floor of your greenhouse—whether it is of gravel, astroturf, or concrete. All this is primarily to clean up the greenhouse before you put in your first crop or at a time when the greenhouse is shut down—when you have been on a vacation, for example.

Captan an All-purpose Disinfectant

Now let me tell you a little more about captan. This is a general fungicide—very effective even for athlete's foot, for example.

I was limping around the greenhouse one day and finally said to my nervous wife, "I'm going home." She said, "No, you're not. You're going to stay here and work." I started crying and telling her my feet hurt. She said, "From what?" I said, "I guess I've developed athlete's foot."

She didn't say any more. She put a couple of tablespoons of captan in a dishpan and said, "Sit over there on that rock, take off your boots and stick your feet in there for about 15 minutes." I said, "You've got to be kidding." She said, "No, I'm not kidding. I want you to stay here the rest of the day and help me." Well, it was really a soothing treatment and I did stick around to help her!

For use on plants I use eight teaspoonfuls to a gallon of water. Put that in your Hudson sprayer and apply it, or you can put it in a sprinkling can and apply it that way. Or, for that matter, you can dip things in it. It is non-toxic to plants, animals, and to human beings, used as directed.

At transplanting time, it is especially helpful. It is a

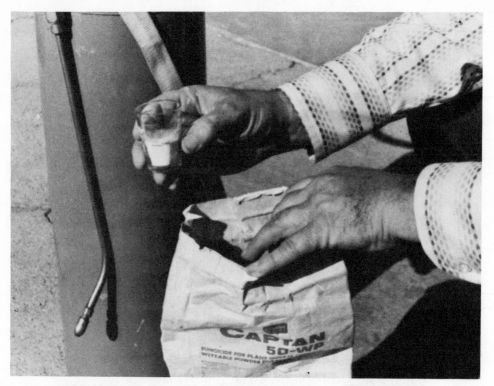

Author illustrates the careful measurement of even a mild disinfectant like captan for use in a Hudson sprayer—medicine cup measurements!

good idea to spray your growing trays with it before transplanting. I also rinse my hands in it just before I handle seeds. And even though I have sterilized the gravel, if I should get it wet I sprinkle captan over the wet area because water mold could be present. (Incidentally, what are some water molds? Two of them are pythium and phytophthora. We sometimes call them damping-off diseases. Of course, in place of using even captan on damping-off, it is better to just avoid getting things too wet in the first place. Prevention again.

The principles of sanitation apply to everything you do in hydroponic gardening. Even the regular changing of your nutrient solutions, as we discussed earlier, is related to sanitation.

You are going to be changing the solution; you are going to be cleaning the tank, because some sulphides can concentrate there. And you don't need them, do you? They can cause a problem in producing too much nutritional stimulation. It will be one of the factors affecting your production.

So when you clean out the nutrient tank, what are you going to do with the waste nutrient? Give it to the trees? Sure. What are you going to use to get it out there? A garden hose? All right. But that garden hose is going to stay outside the greenhouse, isn't it? And you aren't going to use that hose to water the chickens or the birds or the dogs, are you? Why? Because there is going to be some corrosive residue in that hose when you are through with it. After you are through pumping out the nutrient solution, run plain water through it.

There really is much more to learn as you go on in applying all these principles and techniques of sanitation and you will continue to learn with study and practice. Let's have everything in our favor we can, because even then we still have some surprises.

Prevention of Insect Invasions

We have briefly discussed general sanitation measures to keep your hydroponic garden free of various diseases: fungi, molds, mildew, virus and others. But can insects still do you in? Devastate your garden? Well, if you are following good housekeeping procedure you will greatly reduce the chances of that; but what if, despite your best efforts, insects do give you problems? So let's talk about insects.

The thing people ask me about most is aphids. Why is it important to control aphids? Because they carry virus diseases, for one thing. How do you control the aphid? It depends to a great extent on your attitude toward pesticides.

If you think they are usable and necessary, then I would say, "All right, but how about using them before you need them—as a preventative?" And that question does have a simple answer: because you destroy the beneficial insects as well as the aphid. Which ones are they? The ladybug, for one. A green lacewing is another. These insects are going to help a great deal in controlling the aphid.

Now what if the aphid still gets ahead of you? Then you have to use other measures. You have a serious problem. What we are talking about is virus, isn't it? That's our real bug-a-boo—aphid-borne virus.

But let's do this. Let's not do anything to control the aphids. First, let's control the ant. Why do I want to control the ant? Because he spreads the aphid, using it as a source of food. Where do we control the ant? At the ground level. Do insecticides we use on the ant need to get on anything we are going to eat? No. Then can we use chlordane? Yes. So let's use chlordane on the inside and outside wall and control the ant.

This same kind of preventive use of pesticides also applies to the cricket. You knock him out when you knock out the ant and you haven't contaminated your vegetables.

We still don't know whether some pesticides are good or bad. As far as I'm concerned if there is any question about one, let's not use it.

At the same time we need to recognize the great problems facing the growers of food for the masses. Of all the grain that is produced and stored in the United States, how much is devoured by insects? Probably at least a fourth. It is costing every one of us a hundred dollars a year for the loss the consumer has to pay for what the insects eat. So at some point we have to decide who is going to eat, the insects or us.

In this same context we can discuss mice and rats. Even if you don't have any holes around the edges of your greenhouse, are you still likely to find mice in there as the weather turns cooler? Yes, you are. They

Any mice or rats that manage to slip by your greenhouse "security system," can be eliminated with any of the standard preparations, sprinkled along "rat runs"—just don't let pets or small children get to it. Mice (and even pets and children for that matter) are hazards in the greenhouse because of plant disease they may bring in. Children—fine, if they observe the same sanitation precautions you do!

come right up through the ground—unless you have a concrete floor in your greenhouse.

The mice are looking for a warm place. And I'll tell you, if there is something to eat, they eat it. So what do you put there for them to eat? D-Con or D-Rat or other such poison that will really kill them. And where do you put the poison? You put it where it's not going to contaminate anything you use—or along your trays.

Why do we do this? Do we want to keep the old mouse out of there just because of what he may eat? No, it is because he brings in diseases that may destroy our entire crop.

Some people have asked me if one could use cats to control mice in a greenhouse. Well, if you've ever seen a messed up greenhouse, have you ever seen a greenhouse in which a cat had been locked up? I once had to hire help for two days to help me straighten up a greenhouse because a cat got locked inside.

By the time he realizes he is locked up, you know what he starts doing, don't you? He goes on a rampage that you wouldn't believe. Pots knocked off the shelf, plants torn up, plastic coverings ripped. In fact, when I first looked in there, I thought the place had been vandalized. It cost me plenty of money. No cats in the greenhouse for me!

Insect Control With Insect Eaters

Some people seem to control insects with lizards, some with tree toads. I don't like the big toad because he will burrow in my gravel. Also, I once had to fish one out of the nutrient tank and he was highly corroded!

So I don't like toads. I do approve of using lizards, but I recommend that you wash the lizard! Otherwise he may carry in disease. Just dunk them in a little soap—not detergent—solution. Don't ask me to wash the lizard for you because I can't stand the pesky things. But they are good predators. Even a snake is a good predator if that's your bag.

Let me tell you something about chickens. Some nurseries use chickens to control snakes; and, in the Southwest, scorpions—as well as grasshoppers and even mean little kids! They are effective on all of those.

How about the praying mantis? No, don't take the praying mantis into your greenhouse. He is a little hard to wash, for one thing. But you could let its eggs hatch in there. The eggs haven't walked through anything. They are disease-free.

Check locally. Some garden supply places sell praying mantis eggs and predatory insects. Worth looking into.

Healthy Plants vs. Insects

Is it true that insects will not bother a really healthy plant? Well, I do know that nutrition is a factor in preventing infestations. Where you have a high level of magnesium in your plants, for example, you won't be bothered with white fly. I raised the magnesium in my nutrient a lot this year and I don't have the white fly. But of course if the white fly could see what form of magnesium I use, that alone might have driven him off —it's labeled Epsom salts!

It is important to recognize that there are different types of insects that affect plants. There is the primary type and the secondary type. The primary insect will attack a healthy plant. The secondary insect tends to attack a plant that is weakened from disease, storm damage, or an unsealed spot where someone cut off a limb.

But over all this, a more important consideration in insect control in hydroponic gardening is—housekeeping. When a leaf denatures, the plant is through with it. You know that if it discolors, loses its chlorophyl, it is attractive food to some kinds of insects. Go through the greenhouse regularly, remove all that debris and you are not so likely to have insects—or diseases, for that matter.

Plants as Insecticides

We spoke of some insects controlling other insects. Did you know that some plants can help to control insects on behalf of other plants? Pyrethrum, for example —one of the most effective things I've ever heard of. I know a Japanese gardener, unusually successful even for a Japanese gardener—because when he put in his crops, he planted pyrethrum flowers among them. The French African daisy is another; or the French marigold. The daisy, of course, is similar to chrysanthemum in the pyrethrum family. You can put such plants into your crops as a companion crop and they function as a kind of pesticide.

As for some pests such as the cabbage moth, these are so few in a hydroponic garden and so easily detected, you can control them by just picking off the ones you see and throwing them away. As a worm, the moth appears to look something like a measuring worm, a pale-green worm. Just pick them off. Don't use an in-

This type of plant pest is so rare in a hydroponic greenhouse, properly protected, that it is easily controlled just by picking off the few you happen to see. This is the larva of the pandora moth.

secticide. Of course, if you should despite everything get into some major insect problem like a large invasion of white fly, or aphid, where a new batch is hatching every three days, you may have to fight back with an appropriate insecticide.

No Insecticides Recommended

But as a general rule I do not recommend any sprays for the vegetables you will be growing in your hydroponic greenhouse.

I recommend that at a time when your greenhouse is empty, you spray the entire interior, perhaps with Malathion, and that you put chlordane inside and outside the walls to control ants.

We mentioned earlier the value of just washing down your greenhouse interior, perhaps when it is new before you plant anything. Buy a Hudson sprayer or any kind of air-pump sprayer. Buy a brand new one. If you ever made a mistake, it is using a sprayer that had 2-4-D, for example. You just don't wash 2-4-D out of a sprayer, do you? It's there for keeps. Buy a new sprayer and keep it in your bedroom closet or under the bed. No one knows you have it so they aren't going to be tempted to borrow it.

Now put some soap suds or detergent in that sprayer and occasionally wash off the inside of your greenhouse —even with plants growing in it. Why? Well, what's going to collect in that building? Some dust. And what is a red spider? He's a mite, isn't he? And he likes dust. You know, chances are you wouldn't have that insect on some plants if you hosed them down about five times a year with a detergent compound—there would be no place for them to live. But don't forget what I said earlier about a rinsing following the sudsy one to avoid a build-up of film.

Besides keeping the place clean and controlling some insects, you know what? That washdown makes your greenhouse smell terrific. Have you ever been out in a garden right after it rains? Smells great, doesn't it? That's because there is an absence of dust. That helps the hay fever sufferer, too.

What do you do if the mite is already on the plant? What specific insecticide might you try? Malathion. If that won't get the mites, you may have a resistant strain. I recommend that you get in touch with your county agent.

But I do not use Isotox. Isotox is systemic. It penetrates the tissue of plants so that pests that bite the plant will die.

Now how much does a bug weigh? One 10,000th of what I weigh, perhaps? Then a dose that will kill something one 10,000th my size, multiplied by 10,000 will kill what? Me!

In some cases, simply adjusting the pH of your water will affect insects; some are affected by the acidity-alkalinity of the water. When pH will work for plant protection, why reach for the insecticide? Wire worm, for example—check the pH. If it is a high pH, add sulphur or sulphuric acid. The wire worm can't live in a low pH. This is also true of some algae. You can get rid of some algae by changing the pH.

One thing to remember is that we have not only our own insect problems; we have the neighbor's insect problems too, don't we? All around you are buildings and plants that serve as host to many pests and diseases. You can easily demonstrate that just by pouring chlordane-50 around the foundation of your house and watch the sow bugs, ticks, and other crawling, creeping, and flying things emerge! No doubt about it, the foundation of a house or other building is often a host for bugs.

Red spider hosts include junipers, cypress, and oleanders. Do you have any close to you? What can you do about it? Remember the soapy spray. Just wash the dirt off those three plants. Then use a very mild application of insecticide. But wash those junipers, cypress, and oleanders at least three times a year. How much will we cut spider mite population? We will just about eradicate it.

Always think about hosts, and try to avoid moving from handling those right into your greenhouse.

The petunia, for example, is host to many diseases. I have told you about the nasturtium also. Dahlias host many diseases, and I've mentioned the cheese weed, also called button weed or mallow.

Now, when you go into your hydroponic greenhouse to harvest, what are you going to take in order to carry out those beautiful vegetables? A basket, probably. I prefer a wire basket that you can keep clean. Don't take grocery bags into the greenhouse. You will carry all kinds of diseases in on one paper bag. Besides diseases, what could you be carrying in the fold of that paper? Insects, like cockroaches.

Cockroaches are murder. If you do get those, or silverfish, into the greenhouse, there are two or three ways to get rid of them without spraying. Pour two parts of sugar and one part of boric acid into little tubes and lay them around in various places where only the cockroaches or silverfish can get at them. Those pests will start disappearing.

You can also carry nematodes into the greenhouse on pieces of dirt clinging to shovels, dirty tools, or shoes.

Good Housekeeping—Good Results

Practice sanitation, good housekeeping, in your greenhouse constantly. You can't afford the luxury of sharing your food with disease and insects. It's up to you to control them.

Make sure that at least once a year your house is completely out of production. During that time go over

HYDROPONIC GARDENING

every piece of equipment you have, even if you have been checking it continuously anyway. What good is it going to do to control insects and disease if your exhaust fan fails? Think of regular maintenance, too, as a part of your program for plant protection.

Life Is Learning

IN THIS ONE volume is enough information to enable you to begin to enjoy the wonders of hydroponic gardening; to understand the sheer joy of working with living, growing things without some of the usual pains; to experience excellence in the final product; to treasure the rewards of contributing to your family's pleasure and good health.

Beyond this volume, of course, there is much more to learn—about horticulture in general as well as the special field of hydroponic horticulture.

Seek knowledge everywhere. Much that you find in varied works on the starting and training of plants, on greenhouse gardening, on insect and disease control will be helpful in hydroponic gardening as well.

Entire volumes could be written on the cultivation of a single food plant—the tomato, for example. In fact, there are such volumes.

The reader is encouraged to use the libraries available to him, to confer with other gardeners, to broaden his general knowledge of horticulture, and to intelligently adapt that knowledge to the art of hydroponic gardening in his own locality.

The reader is also encouraged to write to the author of this volume with questions and suggestions—to contribute his own experience to future editions of this book.

Also available from the publisher is a periodically updated list of suppliers in the rapidly-growing field of hydroponics. The publisher has no financial interest in any of these suppliers, nor makes any recommendations among them. The information is made available solely for the convenience of the readers of this book.